Cowboy Folk Humor

Cowboy Folk Humor

Life and Laughter in the American West

John O. West

August House / Little Rock
PUBLISHERS

Published by August House, Inc.,
P.O. Box 3223, Little Rock, Arkansas, 72203,
501-372-5450.

Printed in the United States of America

10 9 8 7 6 5 4 3 2

LIBRARY OF CONGRESS CATALOGING-IN-PUBLICATION DATA
West, John O.
Cowboy folk humor: life and laughter in the American West /
John O. West.—1st ed. p. cm.
Includes bibliographical references.
ISBN 0-87483-104-0 (alk. paper): $9.95
1. Cowboys—West (U.S.)—Humor.
2. West (U.S.)—Social life and customs—Humor.
I. Title.
F596.W49 1990
89-18126978—dc20 CIP

First Edition, 1990

Cover illustration by José Cisneros
Cover design by Communication Graphics
Typography by Heritage Publishing Company
Design direction by Ted Parkhurst
Project direction by Hope Coulter
Editorial assistance by Ed Gray

The illustration of the chuckwagon cook pouring coffee is from
Paul Patterson's *Sam Magoo and Texas Too,* and is used here with the
permission of Elmer Kelton and Paul Patterson.
All other illustrations reprinted by permission of NEA, Inc.

This book is printed on archival-quality paper that meets the guidelines for performance and durability of the Committee on Production
Guidelines for Book Longevity of the Council on Library Resources.

AUGUST HOUSE, INC.   PUBLISHERS   LITTLE ROCK

Dedicated to the memories of three teachers—
Bertha Billingslea West, my mother, who opened my eyes to the riches of history;
Everett A. Gillis, who led me into the world of folklore;
and Mody C. Boatright, who stood as a shining example of what a folklorist can be.

Contents

Introduction

I couldn't have been more than six years old when I discovered the fascinating world of the cowboy. I was "helping" Don Bevan, my teenaged next-door neighbor, clean out his family's touring car. Don loved to sing, and from this great distance—over half a century—I remember the tune and most of the words of "When the Work's All Done This Fall."

> A group of jolly cowboys, discussing plans at
>   ease—
> Said one, "I'll tell you something, boys, if you
>   will listen, please.
> I am an old cow-puncher, although I'm dressed
>   in rags;
> I used to be a tough one, boys, and go on great
>   big jags.
>
> But I have got a home, boys, a good one, you all
>   know,

Although I haven't seen it since many years ago.
My mother's heart is breaking, breaking for me,
    that's all,
And I am going to see her when the work's all
    done this fall."

That very night this cowboy went out to stand
    the guard.
The night was dark and stormy, it was raining
    very hard.
The cattle they got frightened and rushed in
    wild stampede,
And Jack [?] he tried to turn them, while riding
    at full speed."

I've forgotten the next couple of verses, but "Jack" (as I remember his name) fell and was trampled by the rampaging steers. The boys carried him back to camp, and then he willed his possessions to them—his pistol, rifle, and saddle. Now, the story concludes, "He won't see his mother when the work's all done this fall."[1]

Thus I was introduced to the hazardous life of the cowboy—doing his duty without regard for danger. Little Joe the Wrangler, I found out many years later, died in the very same way as "Jack"; Jack Thorpe, who wrote Little Joe's song, said it told of a real "Texas stray" who had died on a cattle drive that Thorpe was on.[2] Many a cowboy's reminiscences—not to mention cowboy movies—relate similar tragedies. But the cowboy's life wasn't all excitement and danger.

There were the slack times when days were monotonous and boring—filled with hours of riding fence, checking the cattle for worms and doctoring them with a smelly mixture

10

carried in a bottle in an old cut-off boot top, and even the bane of the horseback cowboy's life, greasing windmills. Such prosaic labor didn't get into the books and movies too often, so it was quite understandable that out in the West Texas town of El Paso, when I was growing up a little later, we all wanted to be cowboys. It was much like Mark Twain and his friends wanting to go steamboating. Several families in the neighborhood had horses, and a few of the youngsters took part in the junior rodeo every year—and not just the wild cow-milking contest, or the greased pig-catching. The rest of us had to be content with dreaming, and making lassoes out of whatever we could come up with, and roping—or trying to rope—anything that was handy: fence posts, cats, dogs, chickens, smaller siblings (sisters, especially). They were not always cooperative, of course, reminding me—many years later—of John Steinbeck's character Tall Bob Smoke, who tried to lasso a stray dog that would squat down and frustrate his efforts as dogcatcher to the point that he tried suicide.[3]

We weren't that easily frustrated; we just kept on trying—and dreaming—of the time when we could ride tall in the saddle. One local yokel-turned-author (who shall be nameless) was reading a cowboy magazine while cocking and uncocking his uncle's .38 caliber revolver—until his thumb slipped and he blew a hole in his knee. For weeks he was the hero of the neighborhood, especially after he reported his first thoughts after the explosion: "He rolled over, and the pistol dropped from his nerveless fingers." As I recall the event, in my imagination I had been involved in a gunfight with the bad guys. Guns and horses and ropes and cowboys: they spelled adventure and excitement. The cowboy was our undying hero, and when Saturdays came, the local movie house always obliged us with not only a cowboy movie, but a twelve- or fifteen-part serial as well. When Hoot Gibson came to town, and I actually shook his hand, my joy was almost complete; at least I couldn't imagine any higher honor.

When I was twelve, the square dance craze came to the neighborhood. Friday nights we went to the schoolhouse and learned to square dance, to schottische, to dance the Varsovienne *(Put your little foot, put your little foot, put your little foot right there . . .)*. Of course we had to dress the part, so I had a red rayon shirt with blue collar and yoke, as well as a pair of real cowboy boots from Sears, Roebuck. I learned to chant out one or two dance calls *(First couple out to the couple on the right, 'round that couple and take a peek, back to the center and swing her cheek . . .)*. And that was pretty close to heaven too. We were doing the dances that real cowboys did, just as we saw in the movies!

This cowboy worship was not, of course, limited to West Texas. Many a boy from the East, after reading of the deeds of daring of Buffalo Bill, Wild Bill, Deadeye Dick, and other intrepid characters, was tempted to run away from home, like Sam Bass, who "first came out to Texas a cowboy for to be."[4] Booth Tarkington's Penrod tried his hand at a novel about "Harold Ramorez, the Road Agent," certainly one result of such reading.[5] Even Billy the Kid, the New Mexican "boy bandit king," inspired several pulp stories and soon rose to the heights of an outlaw pantheon of "saints," of cowboys-turned-outlaw, but really good at heart: they never harmed women, always respected old age, and (like Jesse James) saved poor widows from grasping bankers-about-to-foreclose.[6]

Mody Boatright says that cowboy worship was forged largely by the pulp magazines. The budding movie industry, beginning with *The Great Train Robbery* in 1903, found its true calling with the Broncho Billy series beginning in 1907 and going on to make stars of William S. Hart, Tom Mix, and a host of others over the years. With the arrival of

Gene Autry and other singing cowboys, the genre was reaching its peak—and really drawing in the audiences.[7]

A central part of this worship of cowboys and related outdoor types depicted the recreations of the Old West: songs, often nostalgic ones about the girl left behind, or those about fabulous horses like the Strawberry Roan that nobody could ride,[8] sung to the accompaniment of the guitar around the campfires or in the bunkhouse; telling "windies," or unbelievable yarns, and tall tales of hair-breadth escapes from stampedes, battles with rustlers, crossing rampaging rivers, and fighting Indians; stories of pranks played on the tenderfoot—the list is almost endless. The very nature of such stories encouraged embroidery. In fact, even the truth was often unbelievable.

But cowboy humor was not a luxury; it was a necessity, according to C.L. Sonnichsen, since "our sense of humor helps us bear the unbearable," and "offers escape from boredom on the one hand and from pressure and stress on the other."[9] When you come right down to cases, the boredom lent itself to the story-telling and ballad-singing process, even to the plotting of pranks. Nora Ramírez, who grew up on a New Mexico ranch, recalls that humor enabled the cowboys to survive the monotony of daily ranch activities.

> As a youngster I heard many humorous stories told on the other guy, but it was only as an adult when I talked with my father and other old-timers that I discovered these humorous stories were a necessity in the cattle country. The cowboys stored up in their minds any amusing incidents that brightened their routine chores, and today they bring out these memories for a good laugh when they get together for old times' sake.[10]

13

Paul Patterson recalls from his own early days that because of the hours cowboys spent alone, riding fence or doing other routine chores, "there was time for the telling and retelling, and there was solitude enough for contemplation, and there were rehearsals enough for mastery of the lines."[11]

Such "mastery of the lines" was required of Texas rancher, ranger, and frontiersman Big-Foot Wallace, who was once the guest of honor at a dance while he was visiting his old home in Virginia. When a sweet young thing doubted his story of a herd of horses of "perhaps thirty or forty thousand," which is not entirely impossible, he waxed eloquent:

"Well then," said I, "maybe you won't believe me when I tell you that there is a sort of spider in Texas as big as a peck measure, the bite of which can only be cured by music."

"Oh, yes," she answered, "I believe that's all so, for I have read about them in a book."

Among other "whoppers" I told her there was a "varmint" in Texas, called the "Santa Fe," that was still worse than the tarantula, for the best brass band in the country couldn't cure their sting; that the creature had a hundred legs and a sting on every one of them, besides two large stings in its forked tail, and fangs as big as a rattlesnake's. When they sting you with their legs alone, you might possibly live an hour; when with all their stings, perhaps fifteen or twenty minutes; but when they sting and bite you at the same time, you first turn blue, then yellow, and then a beautiful bottle-green, when your hair all fell out and your finger nails dropped off, and

14

you were dead as a door-nail in five minutes, in spite of all the doctors in America.

Texas residents survived, he told the girl, by chawin' tobacco and drinking whiskey, "and that is the reason the Temperance Society never flourished much in Texas." In fact, Texans even chaw tobacco and drink whiskey in the winter, "when the 'cow-killers' and stinging-lizards are all frozen up!"[12]

Not many people today read *The Adventures of Big-Foot Wallace;* the pulps have dwindled, too—although for some years "breezy" cowboy stories and ranch romances titillated a host of readers. Today's moviegoer yawns through Howard Hughes's *The Outlaw,* in which Billy the Kid and the "full-figured" Rhea (played by Jane Russell), tussling in the hay, once raised eyebrows—and blood pressures—all over the nation. Even so, the rodeo, rapidly becoming a popular attraction, continues to stir up interest in what is by now a bygone era. Reruns of old and not-so-old movies, plus new vehicles such as the *Lonesome Dove* miniseries of 1989, continue to bring back to life aspects of a time that once flourished and still fascinates many a young farm girl or boy as well as the city dweller. The songs, the stories, the adventure and excitement of the cowboy and his life still have an attraction for generations that feel too "fenced in"—who, like Elmer Kelton's "good old boy" Snort Yarnell, long for greener pastures, for

. . . beautiful country. Not spoiled like this country's gettin' to be, but big and wild and wide open. It's like Texas was before they commenced puttin' fences across it and cuttin' it up for farmin'. It's like goin' back to when we was young. [We need to see it] just one more time, while there's a little of it left.[13]

In the windies and tall tales, the pranks and fun, those good old days and that beautiful country live on, at least in the imaginations of the tellers—and those who take time to listen. In fact, as cowboy humorist John Erickson suggests, "ranchers and cowboys may be among the last of our race who have maintained their sense of humor, . . . through courage, determination, and sheer stupidity. There should be some reward for this kind of human tenacity."[14]

And there is a reward—the sheer fun of cowboy humor. Tales about chuck wagon cooks are still good to tell—like the one about the cook that the law got after, and he left "between two days" as the saying went. Well, somebody had to cook, so they drew straws, and whoever got the short straw was elected cook—to serve, by agreement, till somebody complained, when the complainer was to take over. So no matter how bad the chuck was, nobody complained. Finally the cook became desperate to go back to cowboyin', so he loaded up the beans with a double handful of salt. First man to bite into 'em grabbed his throat and hollered, "By God, them's the saltiest beans I ever et!" But about that time he saw the cook taking off his apron, so he added, "But that's just the way I like 'em!"[15]

The recounting of pranks brings its share of the fun, too. Pranks helped fill the cowboy's time, and the tenderfoot was a frequent target. One trick was to wait till the greenhorn was sound asleep, and then wake him abruptly by dragging trace chains over his bedroll and hollering, "Whoa, damn you, whoa!" as if wild horses were loose. Or the more seasoned punchers might haze the tenderfoot with tales of the wild animals about, like the wouser—a varmint that lives only in the folk imagination. They might

even work the old trick of cutting the head off a rattle-snake, then talking the tenderfoot into pinching the tail—knowing that the muscular reaction of the recently killed snake would cause it to "strike" at the person's hand, sending him into spasms of terror.[16] Retelling these incidents—and doubtless, embroidering them ("stretching the blanket")—can be even more delightful than the original event.

And then there are the stories of the damn fool things cowboys would do, like roping the smokestack of a steam locomotive, or a bobcat. One cowgirl even roped a mountain lion and dragged him all the way home![17] Truth or tall tale, the telling is worthwhile.

Such stories are fun to hear today, when the days of the trail herd and the bunkhouse are really a part of those far-off times, the good old days. But these stories lived and were shared because of the long hours of solitude that gave the cowboy time to practice up memorizing and polishing the punch line. After all, as Elmer Kelton could tell us, a good liar needs practice. Many of these bits of humor have been years in the practicing; some I've heard—in a variety of forms and under a variety of circumstances—over the past half-century. Others are "borrowed" bodily (but with permission) from folks such as Elmer Kelton, Curt Brummett, Ray Past, "Doc" Sonnichsen, Paul Patterson, Nora Ramírez, John Erickson, and Joyce Roach. To them, and to countless others who have told me these tales, my undying thanks. I only hope I have managed to tell them in my turn as well as they did.

C H A P T E R   O N E

The Cowboy Talks Funny

The cowboy has always had a language all his own, and it often comes across as odd if not hilarious to the "pilgrims" (as John Wayne called tenderfeet) who don't share his culture. For one thing, he can be plenty profane in his language when "tailing up" a cow that has bogged down in a muddy bottom. Profanity, at such a time, would offer relief to the soul denied even to prayer, as Mark Twain is reported to have observed. But the cowboy didn't talk "dirty" before the ladies, and I wouldn't want to shame my cowpoke friends by quoting them in their bluer explosions.

I remember that when I was a shirttail kid growing up in West Texas, we had a saying that nobody ever used except in "pretend-like." If there was a story behind the saying, it was apparently that a cowboy had turned loose with a "hell" or "damn" without realizing there was a lady present. His speech of apology, which we practiced saying, was far worse than the original outburst: "'Scuse me, lady! I'm a son of a bitch if I saw you. I thought you was a (bleepin') cow!" What it boiled down to was that we had a proverbial kind of response to cover such an occasion, if ever one came up. None ever did, but we were ready.

Real cowboys were generally quite careful about offending the ladies with their speech. I'm reminded of the time Hewey Calloway wakes up in a San Angelo whorehouse in the room of a "wheeligo girl" whom he has paid for services he was too drunk to accept delivery of. Except for an initial "damn" that escapes his lips, he is very polite with her and calls her "honey," but is shocked (now that he's sober) to find that he is "barefoot from heel to forelock" in her presence. Such is the restraint that a good old boy would exercise in the presence of a lady of any level, even under such circumstances.[1]

In another event in Hewey's story, he plays a prank on Fat Gervin, an obnoxious junior banker. All the men—except Fat—enjoy the prank immensely, but unfortunately for Hewey's sense of the fitness of things, the unmarried schoolteacher, Spring Renfro, also sees the incident.

> Hewey noticed the teacher's red dog making his way from one bush, one weed, to another, pausing briefly at certain ones to raise a leg and leave his signature. The boys' black dog followed at a respectful distance, sniffing at each such imprint and endorsing it.
>   Hewey looked over his shoulder toward Fat. The devil began to jab sinfully but deliciously at him. Fat's back was turned, and his jaw was still operating at a hearty pace. Hewey looked toward the house to make sure none of the women were outside to witness his surrender to

temptation. They wouldn't understand. No properly modest woman knew much about male bodily functions, be they animal or human.

He fished a jackknife from his pocket and walked to a tall green weed upon which the red dog's greeting still clung in amber droplets. Carefully he bent over, holding the top of the weed with his left hand while he gingerly sliced through the base, taking pains not to shake it enough to dislodge the drops. Walking as if he were stepping on eggs, he carried it up behind Fat Gervin.

Most of the men were watching Hewey in quiet fascination, but they did not give him away.

He bent and shook the weed, managing to splatter a goodly amount of the dog's scent on the lower part of Fat's left trouser leg, at about ankle level. Fat was so busy talking that he never noticed. He might have wondered why Alvin Loudermilk so suddenly turned around and covered his face, or why the dour Dutchman, Schneider, smiled, but he never let it interfere with the point he was making that most of the progress in this country resulted from the selfless generosity of a noble bank.

That had been the extent of the prank insofar as Hewey had envisioned it. In his own quiet way he had made a statement about Fat Gervin without Fat even knowing about it.

Hewey hadn't considered the black dog. That innocent animal, which had followed Hewey's strange motions with curiosity, sniffed at Fat Gervin's trousers, found there an invitation, hoisted his leg and saluted.

First startled, then enraged, Fat let out an oath
that would have blistered the ears of the wom-
enfolk if they had been outside to hear. He
fetched the black dog a savage kick that sent
the bewildered animal flying. As the dog ran off
howling in surprise and pain, Fat tried in vain to
shake the shame from his trousers.

Alvin Loudermilk was doubled over, slapping
his knee uncontrollably and gasping for breath.
Pierson Phelps had choked on his pipe. Team-
ster Blue Hannigan got up and walked over to
the house, leaning against it with his back
turned, his shoulders bouncing. The Mexican
laughed aloud, which added to Fat Gervin's
rage.

Turning, Fat saw Hewey standing behind him,
trying for Alvin Loudermilk's saintly expression
of infant innocence. Fat seemed to sense that
Hewey might be in some way the author of his
embarrassment. The suspicion deepened, and he
clenched his fists. His eyes strained from their
sockets.

Hewey blinked in bland curiosity as if he had
missed the whole thing.

Hewey's delight was dampened when he learned, moments later, that Fat was in charge of Hewey's brother's
note at the bank, soon to come due and likely to be in need
of mercy. Much worse at the moment was his finding out
not only that the schoolteacher had been looking out the
window and had seen the whole event unfold, but that she
"was tickled to death. In all my life," she said, "I never saw
a more befitting gesture."[2]

Nora Ramírez remembers a couple of stories about profanity out of her ranching past—one a story her father told her about an awkward moment he had endured years before:

> About 5:00 one evenin' Dad called me up and told me to bring five horses to him. He said he'd meet me. I had to tail the horses [tie them to each other by their tails]. Dad and his girlfriend were waitin' for me in the car and just as I got near with them horses, he turned on the car lights. The horses got excited and got all tangled up. I started cussin' Dad out. He knew better than to turn them lights on like that. When I finally got the horses settled down and untangled, Dad asked me to eat supper with him and the woman. "Not after I cussed like I did around that lady," I replied.

And from her own experiences comes a story that suggests the gentlemanly code of the cowboy applied mostly to strange women—not one's own:

> One day a friend of Daddy's drove up and Daddy went out to meet him, swearing occasionally in the course of the conversation. Then Daddy discovered a woman was in the car. He went back into the house with his visitor and the woman stayed in the car. "Why didn't you tell me there was a woman with you?" he asked. "I would have been a little more careful of what I said." After the man left, Mother made a comment to the effect that she, too, was a woman

but she never noticed that it made much difference in Daddy's choice of words.[3]

Although such a qualified bit of evidence muddies the waters somewhat, I must question the validity of a traveling anecdote I have known nearly all my life. As I first heard it, it involved a wild entry in a Carnation Milk Company slogan contest; only in recent years have I read—and forgotten where—the set-up for the story. As the complete story goes, a cowpoke was heading for town one day, and as custom demanded, stopped by ranch headquarters to see if anyone there needed him to pick up something. The boss's daughter had a letter she wanted to have mailed, so he obliged by taking it with him. She hadn't sealed the letter, and being curious the cowboy opened it and read her entry in the Carnation contest. It read,

> "Carnation's the best milk in the land,
> Comes ready to use in a little red can."

When after several weeks had passed and the girl had received no response from her entry, which she *knew* was a winner, she asked the cowboy if he had remembered to mail it for her. He assured her he had done as requested, but admitted that he figured it lacked zip, so he had added a couple of lines:

> "No tits to pull, no hay to pitch,
> Just punch two holes in the son of a bitch!"

As I first heard it, the slogan had won first place with the judges, but the Carnation company couldn't use it.[4] I always thought the company was a bit too puritanical in its decision. Such a slogan would have added a lot of color to their advertising. But it is inconceivable that a hired hand would have used such words to a lady—and the boss's daughter to boot! No cowboy would have done such a thing.

With the disclaimer that the cowboy did talk "salty" when the circumstances demanded, but tried otherwise to sound like a gentleman, the "funny" way he had of expressing himself can proceed. Perhaps the first item on the docket should be what he called himself. The term "cowpuncher," according to old-time trail driver John Young, was a fellow who rode in a cattle car, using a long pole to punch steers that got down, to make them get up before they were trampled.[5] But Paul Patterson and Elmer Kelton, who grew up working cattle in West Texas in the 1930s and 1940s, respectively, said that by the time they came along, cowpuncher was in general use, but the term "cowboy" was reserved as a name of respect for the *real* cowboys—the top hands.[6] Yet in early Texas history, "cow-boy" was often a term of contempt, reserved for hell-raisers who raided Mexican ranches across the Rio Grande, plundered out-of-the-way settlements, and caused problems generally; the label was also applied without reproach to "mustangers" who went out trapping and taming wild horses.[7] Along the Mexican border, *"vaquero"* was common because of the frequent use of Spanish in the region; farther north, in Montana, "buckaroo" is used more often—an odd circumstance, since the word is apparently a corruption of *"vaquero."*[8] These days, of course, the term "cowboy" can be positive or negative—more likely the former with insiders, the latter with others, such as dance hall girls whose toes have just been stepped on. "Waddie" is a term of more recent vintage, especially used in the Wyoming/Montana area (witness "Waddie" Mitchell, the cowboy poet).

Food is always of interest to human beings, and for those whose days of labor are long and lonely, it is of first importance. It is easy to imagine that the cowboy has a colorful—and often hilarious—variety of terms to apply to what he eats. Salt pork becomes "double-breasted ham,"[9] "sow belly, hog side, sow bosom, and pig's vest with buttons."[10] Frijole beans, the cowboy's constant companion, were called "West Texas strawberries,"[11] "whistleberries," or worse;[12] an oyster (if a cowboy ever saw one) was a "sea plum."[13] Bacon, seldom eaten on the trail because it became rancid so easily without refrigeration, was often called—sarcastically—"Fried chicken, chuck wagon chicken, or Kansas City fish."[14] A meal that any chuck wagon cook could make, with whatever ingredients he had available (excepting horns, hoof, and hide of a steer), was in polite society "son-of-a-gun stew," but otherwise by its more natural name—supposedly acquired by the first cowboy who tasted it, who hollered out, "Son of a bitch, but that's good!"[15] Ramon Adams, cowboy historian and linguist, also notes the tendency for an outfit to call the dish by the name of some enemy—"a subtle way of calling him names which one dared not do to his face."[16] (The cook came in for his assortment of names, to be considered later.) And whiskey, that indispensable medication in cases of snakebite or other calamity—if one arose—might be called

> wake-robin, . . . bottled courage, bug juice, gut warmer, neck-oil, nose-paint, and wild mare's milk. Circumlocutions for drinking include "laying on a little more kindling wood," "wetting the whistle," "laying the dust," "crooking the arm," or, in extreme cases, "wearing calluses on the elbow."[17]

John R. Erickson, some years back, published a piece in a

rodeo sports newspaper that brings together a number of flavorful cowboy language examples:

I have spent many pleasant hours listening to cowboys talk, and I have observed the same playful approach to language that Ramon Adams discovered in cow camps and bunkhouses before World War II, and which he recorded in his *Western Words*. The ranching business has undergone many changes since Adams's day, but this one aspect of cowboy life has endured. The cowboys I have known and worked with continue to play with language, to invent words and phrases, and to find new and outlandish ways of describing the mundane and the commonplace. . . .

As an expression of contempt, how about this: "He ain't worth eight eggs." Or, "He had license to be pretty sorry." Or this: "I'd like to buy him for what he's worth and sell him for what he thinks he's worth."

Here's a cowboy's description of his spendthrift son: "If you put a dollar bill in one pocket and a wildcat in the other, I don't know which would get out first."

And here is something an ornery old cowboy told my four-year-old son: "Most folks smell with their noses and run with their feet. But I was made backwards. My feet smell and my nose runs."

Here is a cowboy's comment on the state of the economy: "If you see a rabbit and no one is chasing him, times ain't too bad."

. . . Sandy Hagar on the YL Ranch in Oklahoma was one of those men who built and invented language, and he did it with only a seventh-grade education. Sandy rolled his own Prince Albert cigarettes, which he called "hot tamales." A cigarette butt was a "snipe," and when he ran out of P.A. he poked through the ashtray and went "snipe hunting." In his vernacular chewing tobacco was "ambir" and Joe Blow became "Pete Endgate." He called baby food "grow-pup," and listened to the weather report on the "radiator." On a hot summer day he cooled off in front of the "air commissioner."

Here is a gem of cowboy understatement which was much admired and passed around in the Oklahoma Panhandle. A cowboy (we'll call him Glen) got bucked off his horse and had to go to a chiropractor to get his neck straightened. He hobbled into the office and the doctor asked him what on earth had happened. Old Glen was too proud to admit that he had been planted in a sandhill, so he said, "Well, my horse went down and stepped on my hat."

The chiropractor frowned. "Stepped on your hat?"

"Yeah. My head was in it."

But the real masterpiece of cowboy understatement comes from the Texas Panhandle. Late one night a cowboy was driving home to the ranch, perhaps with a few beers under his belt. He fell asleep at the wheel and rammed his pickup into a bridge abutment. The pickup spun around several times and came to rest out in the pasture.

Bleeding and battered, the cowboy walked to the nearest house and hammered on the door

28

until he roused his neighbors out of bed. The rancher opened the door and stared at the injured man on the porch.

"My God, Jim, what happened?"

"Oh," the cowboy replied, "my pickup quit on me."[18]

The most ordinary everyday items acquired new names in cowboy language, perhaps, as Erickson suggests, to escape boredom. In Paul Patterson's youth, cow chips (used for fire when no wood was available) were called "grassolene,"[19] and the toilet was called an "indoor outhouse," "squat pot," or "indoor flush." His father's name for it, "privy," was frowned upon, and Paul says the four-letter word was never used as part of the title for this accommodation.[20]

Folk comparisons are frequently found in the culture of a group, and the cowboy was certainly no exception to the practice. Will S. James, who after twenty-seven years of cowboying turned to preaching the Word, recorded several good ones:

If an animal was good blood, it was as "fine as split silk." If one was willing to stand by a fellow in trouble, he would stand by him "as long as there was a button on Jabe's coat." If one was lost "he didn't know straight up"; if drunk, "he couldn't hit the ground with his hat"—"as drunk as a biled owl." If a man was homely he was as ugly as "galvanized sin"; if he was rascally, he was "a double back-action, adjustable fraud," "as dirty as a flop-eared hound" . . . if worthless, "he wasn't worth a barrel of shucks"; if lazy, he was "too slow to grow fast," "molasses wouldn't run down his legs."[21]

As Erickson points out, another language habit of the cowboy was understatement—the technique of avoiding saying the obvious without outright lying. Paul Patterson tells of a particularly difficult horse his brother John was trying to break:

> "John," asked a neighbor, "how's that thoroughbred coming along?"
> "Well, he keeps us in the air most of the time, but he's a-comin' along nice!"
> . . . Once in the Marfa country a cowboy was asked if he'd ever slept cold. "No," he said, "I've never slep' cold—but I've laid awake cold a hell of a lot of nights."[22]

The cowboy's life was indeed hard! If only he'd lived in civilized country, where there are houses and an abundance of hound dogs. Then if he got cold, he could just "pull up another dawg."

And then there's the old chestnut I've heard everywhere, about the cowboy who comes in to camp late on roundup. About good daylight when the cook bangs a stirring spoon on a pot to rouse all hands, the cowpoke swears he's just closed his eyes: "Shore don't take long to spend the night around this outfit."

For directness of impact, however, it would be difficult to beat this description of some alkali water, notorious for its bad taste and general undesirable effects: One cowpoke said, "It would give a kildee that flew over it the diarrhea."[23]

Now, that is powerful alkali water.

A humorous incident can bring to life an expression that becomes traditional, finding usefulness in a variety of situations. One such is supposed to have come about when a bunch of cowboys were standing around on a street corner in a Western town.

> . . . A little black dog came trotting across the public square; they were making some very unkind remarks about the dog, as he had no tail and his ears were cut off. An old drunken fellow standing holding to a sign post took in the situation and in his half-drunken, foolish way said: "Something seldom about that little black pup." This created quite a deal of mirth; the boys took it up from that and today there is not an expression more universally in use in the West among the boys than this one, "Something seldom," and the variety of uses to which this expression is subject is something curious; for instance, if one sees a very fat horse "there is something seldom about that horse," if very poor, "something seldom about him," if very large or small it is the same. If a young lady is handsome, "something seldom about that girl," if very homely, "something seldom."[24]

Whether the origin of the term is accurately related or not, the widespread use of it cannot be denied; perhaps its utility is the result of its being flexible, applicable to any situation that might be difficult to describe in ordinary language. There's truly something seldom about that saying!

For a windup, the use of Spanish among cowboys, partly because of the association of Texas cowboying terms with Mexican origins and partly because so many cowboys grow up speaking two languages—at least in Texas—produces this gem, typical of many bilingual anecdotes:

> Alvin Reed tells of the old-timer on the border mighty anxious to find a lost horse. That is, he left not a stone—or a phrase—unturned to find the critter. To everyone he'd meet: *"Oiga,* say, have you seen a *caballo* horse going down the *camino* road with a *mecate* rope around his *pescuezo* neck?"[25]

To a Southwesterner, both this situation and the linguistic richness thereof are just as natural as breathing. The cowboy does, indeed, talk funny.

CHAPTER TWO

Tall Tales

Readers who are not paying close attention might think that cowboys are given to stretching the blanket—in plain prose, to *lying*. Such a belief is far from factual, however. If the cowboy embroiders reality to an excessive degree, he is merely attempting to place the everyday life of the cowhand in proper perspective. In fact, the art of lying is gained only through years of careful study and practice. Mody Boatright, who has made a lengthy and serious consideration of the matter, has expressed his findings clearly:

No old-time cowboy would expect to amuse
you by saying that the outfit he worked for
owned a billion acres of land, as gross an over-

statement as that would be. He would say that
they used the state of Arizona for a calf pasture;
that it took three days to ride from the yard gate
to the front gallery; that the range reached so
far that the sun set between headquarters and
the west line camp. The folk humorist did not
say of a hero that he had the strength of ten
because of his pure heart or because of his im-
pure whisky. He detailed concretely what the
hero would do: he would fight a rattlesnake with
his bare hands and give the snake three bites to
start with. . . .

The tall tale is logical in all points but one. It
begins plausibly and builds to a climax, and the
narrative must not topple until the climax is
reached. . . . One of the old JA hands went to
Arizona and acquired a small ranch on the rim
of the Grand Canyon. One day he was riding
along the rimrock looking out for steers. The
fool bronc he was riding, just out of pure orneri-
ness, he reckoned, bogged his head and began
pitching. The next thing he knew they had gone
off the precipice. Well, when that horse hit the
bottom he just naturally splattered all over the
scenery.

"And what happened to the rider?"

Well, when they went off that rimrock together he knew that that saddle he had been
trying so hard to stay in was no place for him;
so he got off, and he had to be damn quick
about it, for he wasn't more than off the brute
till he hit the bottom.[1]

Precisely fitting Boatright's recipe for lying is a tale Frank

Dobie told about a "tenderfoot spouting about what a monstrous herd he had helped drive." An old cowman kept silent until someone asked about his experience along that line. "I don't remember exactly," he replied, "but it was so big it took us three days and nights every morning to get it off the bed grounds."[2]

The range and variety of the tall tale, of course, are almost endless. The weather, especially out West, always provides plenty of subject matter. The wind is always present on the plains—except that according to a cowboy from eastern Colorado there was so little wind one year that they had to shut off four of their eight windmills. But when the wind did blow, it really blew, especially in Wyoming, where they used log chains suspended from the corner of the bunkhouse porch for windsocks: when the chain stood out straight, they knew the wind was blowing; when the chain snapped off, they figured the wind had gotten up more than usual, maybe to gale force. Up there they never had to turn the windmills off.[3] In one windy story Sam Magoo's friend Willie Wilson swore that

> one morning on the Circle 70's he was standing
> watching a cloud bank up in the northwest
> when *zzzzzzzttttttt!* A cyclone spun up and
> wheeled Willie around with such momentum he
> dug the Circle 70's a hundred and seventy-five
> foot well. Knowing Willie like Sam and I do we
> take that story with a grain of salt. Sam doubts if
> the well Willie made was an inch over a hun-
> dred foot deep.[4]

That well was plenty welcome, because West Texas was the driest place you ever saw: one old-timer says, "When it rained forty days and forty nights, back there in Noah's time, we only got half an inch."[5] Other places didn't do even that well some years. One cowman's wife made efficient use of what she had, however: "Water was so scarce she washed all the children in the same hatful and then threw it on the roots of a spindly shade tree she was trying to keep alive in the front yard."[6]

The changeableness of the weather is often the subject of tall tales. I grew up with the standard line, "Don't like the weather? Wait a few minutes; it'll change." The Crazy Sheepherder Mountains had "the freakiest weather on earth," where the weather could change so quick "the coffee would freeze before it quit boiling. Steam would come off the ice for thirty minutes. One of the herders fainted from sunstroke and then froze to death before he hit the ground."[7] One of the weather tales I heard as a kid was of a bunch of frogs sitting on a pond bank croaking when a norther blew up; an enterprising fellow, timing the arrival of the norther to a fraction, clapped his hands and frightened the frogs; they all jumped for the water—which froze just as they entered it. The fellow mowed them off just above the ice and had a delicious meal of frog legs.[8] Probably more general in its distribution is the following:

One day in January a man was riding across a Texas prairie. He was riding slowly; nevertheless his horse was wet with sweat. The man knew that the day was a "weather breeder" and he kept glancing backward to the north. He was still some ten miles from home when he saw what he had been expecting to see—a low-hanging blue cloud which announced the rapid approach of a wet norther.

There was no house near in which he might

take shelter, but as he was riding a good horse, he hoped to outrun the storm. He "pushed on the reins" and the horse was soon doing his best. In an incredibly short time the ten miles had been covered and the man had not felt the icy wind. As the horse plunged into the stable door, his head, neck and shoulders were in a lather of sweat, but his hindquarters and the man's coattails were covered with ice.[9]

Tall tales frequently circulate about a folk hero who does fabulous things. One such is the cowboy Pecos Bill, who fills a number of pages in Mody Boatright's *Tall Tales from Texas;* the book is structured as a running tale-telling contest aimed at educating a greenhorn named Lanky. Bill, according to some stories, was raised by coyotes, but after he discovered that he had no tail (and was therefore a human), he turned to cowboying. In fact,

"it was him," said Hank, "that invented ropin'. He had a rope that reached from the Rio Grande to the Big Bow, and he shore did swing a mean loop. . . . He roped everything he ever seen: bears and wolves and panthers, elk and buffalo. The first time he seen a train, he thought it was some kind of varmint, and damn me if he didn't sling a loop over it and dang near wreck the thing."

Bill's horse, Widow-Maker, was fed "on a special diet of nitroglycerin and barbed wire, which made him very tough and also very ornery when anybody tried to handle him but Bill." Widow-Maker was a one-man horse, and when Bill finally gave in and let a friend try to ride him, the horse pitched the friend clear up to Pike's Peak, and Bill had to rescue him with that long rope of his.[10]

Bill was not one to be bothered by the lack of rainfall. During one drought he "lit in and dug the Rio Grande and ditched water from the Gulf of Mexico." In another man-sized project he undertook to fence the right-of-way for the Southern Pacific railroad, buying up a bunch of "dry holes old Bob Sanford had made . . . trying to get water. He pulled 'em up and sawed 'em into two-foot lengths for post-holes."[11]

Bill's first wife, Slue-Foot Sue, brought about her own downfall. Against all advice she insisted on riding Widow-Maker—while wearing a steel spring bustle in the bargain. As Joe tells the story,

> . . . she got on that hoss, and he give about two jumps, and she left the saddle. He throwed her so high that she had to duck as she went up to keep from bumpin' her head on the moon. Then she come down, landin' right on that steel bustle, and that made her bounce up jest as high, nearly, as she had went before. Well, she jest kept on bouncin' like that for ten days and nights, and finally Bill had to shoot her to keep her from starvin' to death. It nearly broke his heart. That was the only time Bill had ever been known to shed tears, and he was so tore up that he wouldn't have nothin' to do with a woman for two weeks.[12]

In the Disney version Bill tries to lasso her, but Widow-

Maker is jealous and steps on Bill's rope, making him miss—the only time, of course, that Bill ever failed to rope his target.[13] I really prefer the way Joe tells the story; it's closer to the spirit of the tall tale, especially with the casual way Bill shoots Sue to keep her from starving! The detail fits Boatright's observation about how the climax should be handled; even that situation is solved in a completely logical manner.

Pecos Bill, of course, is not the only phenomenal cowboy around. One pioneer in the Greenbelt region of Texas, A.V. Cocke, winner of blue ribbons for shooting in his younger days, was the subject of many stories about great marksmen, but as he grew older he complained that he couldn't see very well—perhaps in order to lure someone into a contest. One of the spit-and-whittle crew nearby said, "No, he can't see a thing anymore. He can't tell if it's a housefly or a horsefly sitting down yonder on the courthouse."[14]

Then there's the fast roper, Dick Rimmer, who supposedly used to herd cattle out on the Pecos. One of his admirers had to admit he'd never really seen Rimmer rope a calf, but "had seen him milk an antelope on the run in a washtub and not spill a drop." Anybody who's that fast just has to be a fast roper.[15] Not so fast, but certainly plenty tough, is the subject of another short tale:

Riding out on the range one day, a cowhand came upon a rattlesnake. His horse got excited, started pitching, and took off on a wild stampede. They hadn't gone far when they came to a barbed-wire fence, where the horse made a sharp turn, throwing the cowboy astraddle the top wire. The horse was going so fast when he threw the cowboy, and the barbs were so sharp, that he was split clear up to his Adam's apple.

Not to be fazed, the cowboy got up, lengthened his stirrups to fit his situation, and continued on his journey.[16]

Not all mishaps are so easily adjusted to. Pity the poor cowboy who was caught in a dusty roundup situation:

> Years ago some cowboys were branding in the old Salero corral. The dust was so damn thick you couldn't tell a calf from a cowboy.
> The branding and ear marking was going fast so that they could get into camp by dusk. After they finished and the dust began to settle down a little, one cowboy lifted his hand to scratch his ear and to his surprise, he didn't have any![17]

Things could have been worse, as illustrated by a tale Sam Magoo heard from Willie Wilson, who like most cowboys had no use for sheep-herders:

> Back in Indian days three herders stayed together in order to guard the flock day and night. It happened that one herder was blind, one was bald-headed and the other was as normal as was possible for a herder to be. At night they would take time and time about sleeping and standing guard.
> One pitch dark night while the bald-headed and blind ones were snoring in their teepees, and the normal one was on guard, a terrible thing happened. Not only a terrible thing but a

confusing thing took place. Under cover of darkness the Indians scalped the blind herder and took out the bald-headed one's eyes. Well, the herder on guard noticed by the Big Dipper that it was exactly three minutes and thirty-three seconds until the hour of 3:00 a.m.—time for Baldy to go on guard.

When he waked the bald-headed one up Baldy found out he couldn't see. "Heck," he says, "you've went and woke the blind man up instid of me." However, about that time he happened to feel his bald head and says, "By goodness, I guess you've woke us both up." About this time, the blind one, fresh scalped, waked up. He felt his raw skull and says, "Nope, you haven't woke me up. I know I ain't blind and bald-headed both."

I and Sam don't much believe the above story, and you all wouldn't either if you knew Willie like we do.[18]

Frankly, I don't see what they're complaining about; the story seems perfectly logical to me, but then I'm still waiting for the climax Boatright says is necessary.

The cowboy's tall tales often involved animals of a wide assortment. Snakes in particular held center stage. One story tells of Allen Peters, who came across a snake so big "it left a trail the width of a full cotton sack, and jerked Allen's horse down, and broke a new lariat when he roped it."[19] That's a pretty tall one, but nothing like Uncle Jerry's musical snake.

Uncle Jerry was a stubborn old coot who
refused to give in to a long, long drought. He

turned down all offers to buy his place, just stayed there, sitting around on his front porch and playing the harmonica, keeping in practice for the cowboy dances he was often called on to provide music for.

Well, one hot afternoon in June, just before sundown, . . . he had just swung into "The Stars and Stripes Forever" when he happened to glance down at his feet—and there coiled up, with his big wicked head swaying to the music, was the biggest, blackest diamond-back rattle-snake Uncle Jerry had ever laid eyes on. He swore later that it was seven feet long if it was an inch.

The snake enjoyed all the pieces Uncle Jerry played, but he noticed that it especially responded to "Stars and Stripes." The rattler returned every afternoon for the daily concert, and "Stars and Stripes" was always repeated several times each day.

The old boy became attached to the snake, and named him J.P. Sousa, after the composer of the snake's favorite tune. . . . He seemed to really get a kick out of "Stars and Stripes." He even learned to "rattle his rattlers" in time to the music, and thereafter an enthusiastic duet was indulged in.

One afternoon J.P. Sousa failed to show up. Uncle Jerry tried to play, but his heart wasn't in it. It was just like an orchestra trying to play to an empty auditorium. Uncle Jerry hopefully kept an eye open for J.P., but finally gave him up for gone. After that, there were no more evening concerts.

Finally the drought broke, and a neighbor

wanted to lease some of Uncle Jerry's land for
his own herd. They drove out in a buckboard to
search out the best grazing areas.

They were bouncing along, and as they
neared a little hill, the sound of martial music
came to their ears. It sounded a little familiar to
Jerry, so he jerked his team to a halt, and scrambled out of the wagon, and started up the rise,
as fast as his arthritic joints would allow.

When he finally reached the top, a strange
sight met his eyes. On top of the hill was a big,
flat rock. And on this rock were twenty-eight
big diamond-back rattlers, grouped in a circle. In
the center, his head waving proudly, and his
rattles beating out the time just a little louder
than the rest, was old J.P. Sousa, leading his musicians in a loud but positive rendition of "The
Stars and Stripes Forever."[20]

I'm certainly not surprised at old J.P.'s choice of music. I
think it's one of the very best marches Sousa ever wrote.
Wouldn't you give a purty to hear that rattlesnake band? I
sure would.

Frank Dobie was fascinated with rattlesnakes, writing a
whole book on the subject—natural history, windies, and
factual experiences. The following is told as truth, but the
reader might come to a different decision. An old rancher
once told Dobie,

Well, I saw something once concerning rattlesnakes that I never expect to see again. It was
out in the Davis Mountains country and I was
just a kid. One day I rode up on two rattlesnakes

43

swallowing each other. Each was about three feet long and they had each other by the tail. They had swallowed so far that each snake was actually beginning to swallow itself. I sat there on my horse watching them maybe fifteen minutes and all the time the hoop they made was getting smaller and smaller. After a while I got down and killed them. I have always regretted that I did not let them finish swallowing and then bring them in to preserve in alcohol. They would be quite a curiosity.

Dobie had an interesting response to the story: "Personally I have no doubt that they would have gone on swallowing until nothing but the heads were left and the circle reduced to a dot. Any of the higher mathematicians that figure on infinity can understand the proposition." Clearly, Frank Dobie had a sense of humor. In fact, he went on to tell the rancher that the story reminded him of two wildcats doing battle:

Every time one of them jumped on the other, the under one jumped out and mounted the one that was on top. Exchanging positions that way, they kept on getting higher and higher until the man watching them lost sight of them and would have doubted that they were still progressively fighting if he had not noticed an occasional bit of fur falling at his feet.[21]

The following sequence of events is as logical as Boatright would demand—right down almost to the climax:

44

One of our cowboys was branding calves out on the range and jumped a bear. He took to him on his pony. He pulled his pistol to shoot and just as he did his horse jumped a log and instead of killing the bear he shot his boot heel off, dropped his pistol and lost his hat. He jerked down his rope and caught the bear right around the neck. The bear rose up on his hind feet, caught the rope in his four paws and here he came towards the pony. The cowboy jumped off his horse, and tore off down the mountain. He looked back after running a piece and saw the bear coming. He was sittin' up in the saddle, had the cowboy's hat on, and was making a loop to try and rope him.[22]

Less dramatic—and possibly even true—is the story of a bunch of goats from "down Pecos way" that were being shipped by train to Kansas City. "Lod" Calohan, who was in charge of the shipment, says that he

opened the port holes in the freight cars because I got to feeling sorry for the goats on account of the terrible heat. The next morning I had the surprise of my life. I looked out ahead over the train [from the caboose, probably] and it was white with goats. Those hundreds of goats had climbed up through the port holes during the night and leapin' from car to car, had distributed themselves on the roofs of the box cars. It looked like the top of the train had been strewn with popped corn.
As soon as the train stopped we tried to con-

trol those goats, but having been raised in the
wild hills of Southwest Texas, it was no trick at
all for them to leap from one car top to another
and [they] were soon on tops of cars all over the
yards. It was too far for them to jump to the
ground. It took us four hours to load them back
in their cars.[23]

For variety's sake I'll throw in a couple of stories about
horses, the mainstays of the cowboy's life. Out of his childhood, Tol Rutledge once explained the secret of how he
and his brothers had learned to ride well. He said, "Practice
when you're young. As kids Papa used to mount us out on
stick horses ever' morning. And most of the times they'd
pitch with us for a quarter of a mile or more."[24] Those
phenomenal stick horse were something else, but only a
few horses developed personalities and skills that made
them famous—like "old Bald," subject of a story Joe told
the greenhorn Lanky once:

Tell you what happened once. We'd been
gatherin' the bulls and throwin' them into the
bull pasture and we'd got through and there
wasn't much to do right then, so we was just
kind of layin' around the house, ridin' a little
and keepin' things up, but nothin' very rushin'.
Well, I turned old Bald out thinkin' a few days
rest wouldn't hurt him none. He was as gentle
as a dog and was always comin' around the
bunkhouse every day wantin' me to pet him and
the like. Then one day he didn't come. I knowed
there'd been a hoss thief in the country not long
before and I kind of got worried about him. So

when he didn't come up by the middle of the evenin' I caught me a saddle hoss and thought I'd ride around a bit and see if I could locate him.

I'd rode about five miles, I guess, when I topped a little hill and there was old Bald and a two-year-old gelding down in the valley cuttin' the dangdest didoes you ever saw. Old Bald would go over to a little place and ease around, then he'd wheel off toward the gelding and the gelding would meet him and he'd go back and do the same thing over again. I watched him for a while, mighty sad I was, because I thought he must of et some loco weed. He acted jest like he was cuttin' cattle, only there wasn't any cattle anywheres around.

Then I rode up close and seen what he was doin'. He was on an ant bed, cuttin' the bull ants out of the herd. And he had the gelding holdin' the cut.[25]

I reckon I'd better quit on these tall tales, before somebody thinks I've gone to lying. I wouldn't want that.

CHAPTER THREE

The Cowboy's Pranks

The pranks cowboys play often are as wild as some of the tall tales they tell. The straightfaced humor involved in "loading the greenhorn"—really laying it onto some poor unsuspecting flatlander, or even selling an unsuspecting buyer the same cattle over and over—is a bit hard to swallow sometimes. Yet these stories generally are told for truth, with only a trifle of the usual blanket-stretching involved. I'm reminded of school buddies getting together after a long spell, when some clown always starts off, "You remember the time we . . .," and everybody makes out like he actually *does* remember—but privately knows that the teller is making it up as he goes along. Sometimes it's merely wishful thinking, dreaming "If only we'd been brave enough to really do that . . . ." Dormitory girls who "remember" putting Saran Wrap over the toilet bowl (un-

49

derneath the seat), and the consequences thereunto apper-taining, are in the same category. But cowboys are crazy. They do wild things, remember them with relish, and enjoy retelling them, sober or not. Of such are the following accounts.

Many a Western movie has scenes with the hard-nosed ruffian shooting at the tender feet of tenderfeet, making them dance against their will. I wouldn't say that such never took place, the perversity of humankind being what it is, with the cowboy's propensity for getting wild drunk and disorderly on occasion. But Phil Rollins, who made a study of the genus *Cowboy* back in the 1920s, says that was not a common practice, taking place "extremely rarely." On the other hand, the cowboy often had occasion to feel that tourists considered him to be an object for gawking at, ordering around, and treating like a monkey in a cage. Under such circumstances, the cowboy found ways to scare tourists into seventeen kinds of fits.

In one such event, five cowboys in the town of Pocatello "were doing nothing more 'wild and wooly' than eating canned peaches out of five cans" and visiting with a young girl and her dolly. At that moment a train rolled into the station for a twenty-minute stop.

From one of the Pullmans alighted two young and comely women, a self-confident cub male, and a stout, elderly, austere female.

The young women and the cub male, each carrying a camera and clicking their way among the station's populace of disdainfully inquisitive townsfolk and seemingly imperturbable Indians, came upon the cowboys. Click, click, click, this for a dozen times, and punctuated with "Aren't they interesting!" "Right out of a book!" "I think

TOO EARTHY

that one over there is the most picturesque!"
The punchers did not counter. They merely
writhed and grunted and lessened their talk to
dolly. Then the cub male authoritatively volunteered: "You men move into a straight line. The
ladies want to take you that way." Ed Peters,
one of the quickest shots on the northern
Range, quivered, glanced at the cub male, serious-faced in his position as general manager,
glanced at the young women, serious-faced in
their perpetration of a nuisance, grinned, and
ordered: "Let's get in line, fellers."

Quietly, save for the jingling of spurs and the
scraping of feet, the men moved as requested,
and resignedly were clicked standing, and then
squatting.

The men had not yet risen in compliance with
young cub's next dictum: "Say, this looks too
peaceful. You men draw your guns and brandish
them," when the stout female bustled up in answer to "Mother, come here. We've found five,
real, live cowboys." Mother looked again,
sniffed, said, "I'll have to change my specs,"
looked again and uninterestedly observed:
"Humph. Fancy. They're playing with a doll.
And as for those hairy overalls, they suggest
vermin."

Ed Peters shot out sotto voce to his companions: "My Gawd, ten minutes more of this! Not
on your life." Then he rose to his full height of
six feet three, doffed his wide-brimmed hat with
a courtly flourish, and commenced, with honey
voice: "Beg pardon, ma'am, for speakin'," he
continued, with a howl to his companions,
"Whoop, playing with a doll and full of vermin!

They wants our real selves. Rise up, you murderous devils, and raise immortal hell for the ladies."

The audience fled. The punchers solemnly bowed to their little guest, mounted, and rode out into the lava beds.[1]

A wilder—and swifter—reaction from the wild and woolly cowboys might have been expected.

Not that the cowboy was above teasing the newcomer to test his mettle, or perhaps to cure him from some affliction. One young man who was deathly afraid of panthers joined a bunch of cowpokes around a campfire, who proceeded to recount every scary tale of "conflict between man and panther" they could come up with. He insisted on placing his bedroll between a couple of other men for safety.

One night one of the boys, who could imitate the panther, came into camp rather later than usual, and as he came singing along, within a hundred yards or so he hushed singing, fired off his pistol, squalled like a panther and then began to hollo murder, at the same time dismounting and striking his horse, making him run into camp riderless, while he kept up the most unearthly screams crying for help.

The rest of the boys carried the charade off well, including bringing the "attacked" one in wrapped in a blanket smeared with blood from a beef killed earlier that day. But they couldn't find the victim of the joke!

> They began to be alarmed for him, when they
> discovered him in a tree some thirty or forty
> yards away. . . . They never tried to scare him
> again, and strange as it may seem, after hearing
> that it was a joke he was never afraid of a pan-
> ther again.[2]

In milder cases of hazing the tenderfoot, a rider on a
peaceful horse might be warned that the mount was a bad
bucker notorious for suddenly going wild. Tale-telling
might involve a seemingly endless tale that, ultimately, has
no point at all. Exaggerated stories of wild animals—like
the wouser, which often had hydrophobia—were often
told, and the deceptively clear air of the wide open spaces
led the greenhorn to swallow whole innumerable stories
that a nearby hill or mountain was several miles away.[3]
And to the person unaware that a cow has no upper teeth,
a newcomer who has bought a herd in good faith could
easily be assured that he was swindled, with ancient and
toothless livestock having been passed off on him as
healthy three-year-olds.[4] Frequently the person who took
such ribbing in good spirits became one of the bunch, and
might even be included in pranks played on some of the
old-timers. Such is the case with one greenhorn who was
brash enough to go West wearing a high silk hat. He had
bought a herd of two thousand steers, and came out to take
delivery of them. While there he took a nap under the
shade of a tree to await the chuck wagon cook's call to
dinner; his hat lay by his side.

> Chuck time drew near and the boys, fifteen or
> twenty of them, came riding into camp for the
> purpose of eating something up. As they ap-

54

proached the place where Mr. N. was, the tramp of their horses' feet disturbed his slumbers and when fairly awake he heard the boys, who had stopped within twenty or thirty feet of where he lay, commenting on something. One said "What must we do?" Another said, "What is it?" One said, "It's a bear," another, "It's the venomous kypoote." Another said, "It's one of those things that flee up and down the creek and cry 'walo wahoo,' in the night time." One called out, "Boys, it's a shame to stand peaceably by and see a good man devoured by that varmint," and calling loudly to the now thoroughly excited old man to "Look out there, mister, that thing will bite you," at the same time drawing his pistol. Mr. N. sprang to his feet like a ten-year-old boy (as some of the boys put it, got a ten-cent move on him), and didn't stop to get his hat. He had perhaps gotten ten or fifteen feet . . . when almost every man in the outfit fired (some of them two or three bullets) into that silk hat, simply shooting the crown off.

One of the boys turned the relic over carefully with a stick and assured all around that the critter was dead.

Our good-natured old friend, after recovering from his scare, took a hearty laugh over the little jamboree and called the boys all 'round to his wagon and drew out a jug of sixteen-shooting liquor—thus they celebrated the death of the terrible varmint.

One of the boys loaned the jolly old boy his

hat, and he wore an old one until he could get one from town, when they all chipped in and bought one of the best to be had, a regular cowman's hat, and gave it to Mr. N. . . . But one thing certain, he hadn't been in that outfit three days until every man on the ranch, even to the cook, would have fought his battles for him, if occasion had presented itself.

One of the curiosities of this story lies in the fact that "Mr. N." was so well-preserved that none of the boys realized he was "as old as fifty"—if they had realized that he was so ancient "they would never have 'killed the animal'," out of respect for his age.[5]

Sometimes a newcomer could work his way into acceptance by a group of cowboys by pulling a prank of his own. One neophyte had attempted to dress as a wild and woolly sort with long hair and gruff exterior, but nobody seemed much impressed. Then, one night on duty riding around the herd, the new man passed another cowboy on his route in the other direction. As they passed, the "insider" asked the "outsider" what he was running from when he came West. On the next round, the new man said he'd been accused of stealing. On the next round, what had he stolen? A steamboat. On the last round he admitted that when he went back to steal the river too, they came after him. Such mental agility won the newcomer a place in the bunch![6] Anyone who could lie like that would do to ride the river with.

It took a while for one tenderfoot to find out that he was being fooled by the boys. He had prepared to go "up the trail" to Kansas by buying a complete cowboy outfit, Colt revolver, scabbard, cartridges, and all. When a man named Hill joined the outfit, the youngster was told to look out for

Hill—he was one mean hombre, much given to stealing, and likely to kill on little or no provocation. The boy's matches, cartridge, cigarette papers—anything he had—would turn up missing as time went on, and he "even had to skin prickly pear to get wrappings" for his roll-your-own cigarettes—and of course Hill was the guilty one. The boys assured the newcomer that to complain would be his death. Finally the villain, who was in on the trick, told the tenderfoot that he had been the subject of a prank. "We all had a good laugh and from that time on harmony reigned in camp."[7]

Sometimes a foreigner was the butt of cowboy pranks. There was a period of time when British firms were investing in land and cattle in the American West, and with their "funny" ways of talking and acting, the cowboys had natural targets for their fun. One story involves New Mexico Senator Dorsey and just such a bunch of "eyeglass" Englishmen—stuffy folks who, through their fancy monocles, looked down on cowboys—who bought a large herd of cattle for twenty-five dollars a head. The task remained of delivery, which consisted of counting the cattle as they were driven past a particular spot, both seller and buyer keeping their own tallies of the numbers driven past. The old trick of driving the same cattle round and round a hill was employed. Jack, the foreman, was told to pick out a good place where the trick could not be found out.

Jack selected a little round mountain with a canyon on one side of it. Here on the bank of the canyon he stationed the Englishmen and their bookkeepers and Senator Dorsey. The Senator had only about 1000 cattle, and these Jack and the cowboys separated into two bunches out in the hills. Keeping the herds about a mile apart, they now drove the first herd into the canyon. . . . It was hardly out of sight before the second bunch came stringing along. Meantime the cowboys galloped the first herd around back of the mountain and had them coming down the canyon past the Englishmen for a second count. . . . Thus the good work went on all morning, the Senator and the Englishmen having only a few minutes to snatch a bite and tap fresh bottles.

. . . By about three o'clock in the afternoon the cattle began to get thirsty and footsore. Every critter had already traveled thirty miles that day, and lots of them began to drop out and lie down. In one of the herds was an old yellow steer. He was bobtailed, lophorned, and had a game leg. When for the fifteenth time he limped by the crowd that was counting, milord screwed his eyeglass a little tighter on his eye and says:

"There is more bloody, blarsted, lophorned, bobtailed, yellow crippled brutes than anything else, it seems."

Although the senator had the men try to cut the old steer, old Buck, out of the herd, he escaped them—and continued the circular route he had been practicing.

A week later a cowboy reported finding old Buck dead on his well-worn trail. No one ever rides that way on moonlight nights now, for the cowboys have a tradition that during each full moon old Buck's ghost still limps down the canyon.[8]

Did the Englishmen ever discover the trick, or get fair treatment from the senator? History fails to relate, but those Englishmen were so funny, they probably deserved being tricked that way—except that the Code of the West— a man's word being his bond—makes this into a reversible prank, good for laughing over with plentiful liquid refreshment, once the Englishman is accepted into the category of "folks" despite his curious ways. A good prank is worth all the work entailed, after all.

Gus Black, who went up the trail many times during the 1870s and 1880s, recalled a prank he once played, passing a young yearling off as an old-timer:

One trip Governor Bush came out to meet the herd in company with Captain Lytle, and we entertained him in camp. That morning I had found a couple of long horns which had slipped off the head of a dead cow on the trail, and in a spirit of fun I fitted them onto the just-sprouting horns of a dogie yearling with our drags. That little old yearling was a comic sight with those great long horns on its head, and caused lots of fun for the boys. When Governor Bush was looking over the herd he espied this "long-horned" yearling, and began to hurrah Captain Lytle about the animal. I told the Governor that it was just a yearling, but he said it was a four-year-old, and would bet any amount of money on its age. I told him I would bet $200 it was a yearling. He promptly covered the bet, . . . and then I roped the dogie and we took the horns off. Governor Bush was dumbfounded, and the laugh was on him. When settlement came around, I told him to keep his money, as he was

so d----d ignorant I just wanted to teach him a
lesson. Then he set up the whiskey and cigars to
the outfit.[9]

The long hours with little mental stimulation that the
cowboy endured, mentioned earlier, also gave him opportunity to dream up pranks galore. Even Texas Rangers,
those renowned minions of the law (who were often cowboys at times), had time on their hands for thinking up
devilment. James Gillett, who spent six years with that
body, tells off on the rangers:

During the winter the boys played many tricks
on each other, for there were no Indian raids
during the time we were in this winter camp.
One of the favorite stunts was to extract the
bullet from a cartridge, take out the powder and
wrap it in a rag, and then, while the inmates of a
given cabin would be quietly smoking or reading or talking around their fire, climb up on the
roof and drop the rag down the chimney. When
the powder exploded in the fire the surprised
rangers would fall backwards off their benches,
to the huge glee of the prank player. At other
times a couple of rangers would post themselves
outside a neighbor's cabin and yell "Fire! Fire!"
at the top of their lungs. If the cabin owners did
not stand in the doorway to protect it all the
rangers in camp would rush up and throw bedding, cooking utensils, saddles and bridles, guns
and pistols outside as quickly as they could. In a
jiffy the cabin would be cleaned out and the
victims of the joke would have to lug all their

60

belongings back in again.[10]

The Western artist Charlie Russell, who drew what he knew, having spent years in the West, was capable of pulling a cowboy prank himself. In one account he told of having gotten some Limburger cheese and generally raising havoc therewith: he "rubbed it on doorknobs, bar-rails, beer glasses and hatbands," he reported. Then he found another subject for inclusion in the prank—an old-timer who'd had an overdose of nose-paint. Unfortunately for him, he also had an enormous drooping moustache, which was liberally dosed with the cheese. When he awoke, there was hell to pay:

> "Bill," I says, "how you feelin' this mornin'?"
> "Keep away from me, I'm dyin'," he says, waving me back.
> "What's the matter?" I asks. "You sick, Bill?"
> "No, I've felt as bad as this a thousand times," says Bill, "but this is awful. I'm goin' to die sure 'cause no man can live long with this awful breath. I'm plumb spoiled inside. I'm dyin' sure."[11]

Paul Patterson shares a good one about a cowpoke who had the habit of coming in to town from the outfit where he worked. He would

> tie his horse in front of the first saloon, and proceed to have a look at the elephant and listen to the lobo.

61

One day the boys sneaked out and turned his saddle around. Directly out wobbles the cowboy and climbs into the saddle. But something seems amiss? Nope. Here's the saddle horn. And the stirrups? But hold up, here. Where's Old Rambler's head at? Looking quite confused, not to say abused, the cowboy steps down, reties his horse, steps back and kicks the critter a resounding boot in the belly. "Now, you old so and so! Ain't you ashamed of yoreself? Now stan' there till you sober up!"[12]

Even the clergy came in for a share of tricks from the cowboy—especially when there was a question about the legitimacy of the preacher's actions. One circuit-rider, Parson Brown, had curious habits. Dressed up in a Prince Albert coat, and sporting a cane "made out of that part of a buffalo that makes good canes," he would disappear when the grass started coming up, seldom telling even his family where he was going. After one such absence he returned "wearing a saintly air," saying he had been assisting with a revival meeting. His wife helped make ends meet by running a boardinghouse and providing meals for folks who were in town for the day. A group of cowboys were at dinner when the parson got home, and after he hung up his Prince Albert he went to wash up. One of the group, known for his tricks, left the table and returned shortly, having stopped at the parson's coat. After the meal, the parson noticed that the pockets on the coat were bulging out somewhat, so he investigated. Out came "a long red sock, a deck of cards, and an empty half pint whiskey flask." The boys joshed him pretty thoroughly, asking how much he'd won, and why he hadn't shared the whiskey with them. The parson took the prank well, and so did his wife, who apparently trusted him more than she did the boys![13]

Some cowpokes laid claim to more virtue than they actually had, and a prank could often smoke them out. Lon Hunter, a New Mexico cattleman, enjoyed telling about one such situation:

> One time there was a bunch of us cowpunch-
> ers out on roundup gettin' ready to eat. This one
> feller thought we should ask a blessin' before we
> eat. The others thought it wasn't necessary. That
> night I said to one of the boys, "I don't believe
> that feller has as much religion as he thinks." So
> I dropped a cactus in his boot. Then somebody
> called him and he jumped up out of bed right
> quick and stuck his foot in that boot. He cussed
> a blue streak.[14]

The variety of pranks that cowboys could dream up was wide indeed; some took planning ahead, while others just seemed to happen because there was an opportunity. As one cowboy humorist describes things, "in the heat of the day it's always fun to ride over and put the toe of your boot under the tail of the next man's horse." Or, if the other rider is half asleep, "you can unhook his back cinch or slip the headstall over his horse's ears."[15] Anything to stir up a little excitement at someone else's expense!

Other jokes take more preparation; imagine the training of the horse needed for the following:

> One day Felix Crowhoppie (a sheepherder
> who come over here from France) was standin'

on the street and Dick Raley come ridin' down
that street with a wide, flop hat on. Suddenly
the horse fell over and Dick began shoutin'.
"God, he broke my leg. The horse's leg is broke,
too." Felix was so excited he ran into the nearest store tellin' everyone about the terrible accident that just happened. While he was gone,
Dick got up, tied his red bandana around the
horse's leg and the horse got up and went
around on three legs. When Felix come back
out and saw that horse walkin' around on three
legs he was shore impressed.[16]

Sometimes playing a prank, say to get even with someone, involved self-sacrifice or discomfort on the part of the
prankster—but the resulting revenge was often worth it.
Lon Hunter once was the last man to come up to the Salt
Springs near the Organ Mountains of New Mexico, when
he and a crew were driving a small herd of cattle. A five-
gallon can of rainwater was usually kept in a shack near
the spring, and the other boys, hot and thirsty, drank it all
up, leaving Hunter without any. When he saw they hadn't
saved any for him, he went over to the spring and drank
deeply, pretending to enjoy it. The boys asked him about
the water, and he assured them it was fine—so they drank
plenty too. On the way back home they got so thirsty from
drinking the salt water that they had to go and find some
good water—but Hunter got even with them, even if he
suffered too.[17]

Even life on the trail could be livened up with a little
prank. Frank Dobie tells of Tommie Newsom, who had
crossed the Red River at the famous Doan's Crossing many
times before, although the rest of the crew didn't even
know what the Red looked like. Tommie went ahead to

scout, and he noticed that the river was low, but long bars of white sand in the riverbed looked like water reflecting the sun—so he told the boys the river was on a rampage, and they'd better prepare to swim. He had them strip off their clothes and guns and put them into the chuck wagon, which he took over the river on a round-about route, crossing where they couldn't see. He told them to graze the herd slowly toward the river for an hour, and then try the crossing. As Dobie summed the event up, "what Tommie's cowboys said when they approached the white sands and while they drove on in their undershirt-tails can be better imagined than printed."[18]

Even dances, those welcome breaks in the year's monotony for the cowboy, had a standard prank, often reported by a variety of sources. Owen Wister's Virginian, usually thought of as more serious-minded than most, was guilty of pulling this trick. He had ridden 118 miles to get to the Swintons' barbecue and dance, but when Miss Woods, the schoolteacher, danced with the married men rather than with him, he got even by swapping the blankets on the dozen babies asleep in an adjoining room.[19] As Guy Logsdon, authority on cowboy music and dance, explains, a regional dance attracted folks from miles around, and children were brought along as a matter of course. Since the families had ridden or driven for long distances to get there, they weren't about to quit early and go home. A dance usually went on till all hours, and after it quit the parents gathered up their sleeping children—guided by the familiar quilts and blankets they were wrapped in—and deposited them in the wagons for the ride home. Far too often, if the reminiscences are to be trusted, the kids woke up halfway home (or even later) to discover they had been unwrapped and rewrapped by person or persons unknown, and were going home with the wrong set of parents![20] Paul Patterson recalls that in his early days this trick was so well-known and widely practiced that when a dance was held in the Upland County courthouse, the children were parked for sleeping in the jury room, "each tagged and labeled against baby-switching pranksters."[21]

Curt Brummett, a longtime cowboy who grew up in the saddle near Clovis, New Mexico, must have grazed a bit on loco weed when he was a tad, judging by his memories of childhood and early school days. To hear him tell of his experiences, he was much given to tricks of every variety. The following three stories are all his, and they would seem to prove that playing pranks is a disease that starts young with cowboys and never leaves them. Sometimes the older cowboys infect the younger ones. There is even a slight possibility that Curt has had blanket-embroidery lessons too, but I'll let the reader judge.

Alarm Clocks
BY CURT BRUMMETT

It was spring and school was just about over for the year. School would be out for us about three weeks earlier than for the rest of the kids because of the cattle works. I sure was glad to hear the old man say I could go with 'em this time. Usually I had to wait until school was out and then catch up.

Spring cow works meant six to ten weeks of roundups, branding, roping, and pretty good times. All of this comes in the form of long hard hours a-horseback, flanking calves, and the smell of dust and burnt hair. My two brothers decided that since it was my first time to make the whole works, we needed to leave school in a flash of glory. Yep, we had to pull something special. We discussed burning the schoolhouse

66

down but that was out, and we discussed kid-
napping old Slimtech (the schoolteacher), but we
didn't really want to do anything that would get
somebody hurt—or us caught. So as we were
riding to school one morning and old Slimtech
came to meet us I got a pretty good idea.

Slimtech rode a mule that he had bought from
our dad. Old Lucifer (the mule) had a tendency
to blow up—stampede or go just plumb crazy for
the least of reasons, such as lunch pails rattling
or stovepipes attacking him [another of Curt's
tales involves a stovepipe someone roped,
spooking the mule "a few"]. And anytime something unusual happened and that mule come
apart, it was at least three hours before he could
be calmed down and things even start to get
back to normal. It was old Lucifer that was
gonna help us out. I was so proud of my idea I
didn't even want to share it with anybody, so I
would pull it off by myself. Besides, I had a
score to settle with our local educator.

It seemed that old Slimtech thought that
everything that had happened to him that year
was my fault. And I might add that he had some
kind of memory. Every time we started to eat
lunch he very carefully tasted it, very slowly.
And when riding home to school or from school,
him and old Lucifer always rode at the back of
the group. He rode there so he could keep an
eye out for any practical jokes. He even justified
having me cutting up firewood every day for
the school stove by saying that not only was I
building up my mind, I was building up my
body. The time was getting close to pull my little
trick, and I was so happy I couldn't hardly stand it.

Now old Slimtech kept an alarm clock on his desk so's he could make sure each lesson on each subject had equal time. He would set the alarm clock for a certain length of time and when that set of bells rang, it meant that one subject was done for the day.

Slimtech had a very precise schedule when school was over each day. He would close his books, put them on the shelf, put his lunch pail with the alarm clock in it on the desk, and then go outside to saddle old Lucifer. After making sure everything was put up and everyone was ready to leave (or had already left), he would pick up his lunch pail, leave and lock up the building, tie the pail to old Lucifer, lead him about fifteen to twenty feet to make sure old Lucifer wasn't going to do anything harsh. By harsh I mean try and kick the lunch pail out of the county, or pull a one-critter stampede.

Well, the last day of school for me was upon us, and I was some of that excited. I had my plan timed to perfection. Actually it was quite simple. As my last day was here I volunteered to cut an extra batch of firewood about fifteen minutes before school was out. This act alone caused Slimtech to spill a bottle of ink and go into a minor fit of choking. But just because he was a schoolteacher didn't mean he was dumb. He accepted my offer.

My timing was perfect. I was bringing in a load of firewood just as Slimtech was walking out to saddle old Lucifer. I grabbed the alarm clock, set it for what I thought was five minutes, and put it back in Slimtech's lunch pail. I was leaving to get my horse as Slimtech was coming

68

back inside. He even commented on the fact
that I might someday amount to something. I
mentioned that I was wanting to get going because we were going to leave early the next day
and I had a lot of gear to check out. He grabbed
his lunch pail and came out with me. Tom and
Joe had my horse saddled and ready. They were
grinning something fierce.

Tom said our farewell party was about to be-
gin. They had cut the saddle strings on one side
of the cantle so's that when Lucifer started trot-
ting, the slicker would slip to one side and cause
a mild stampede. I just laughed and said that
wasn't nothing. I told 'em to watch as Slimtech
led old Lucifer out. I figured that clock ought to
go off about the time old Slimtech was ready to
turn around and get mounted. Oh yes—something I failed to mention: until that day I had
never touched an alarm clock. Any hoo, he got
on old Lucifer and we started for home. We had
made about a quarter of a mile and nothing had
happened. The slicker hadn't even slipped. I had
completely given up and was fixing to turn
around and tell Tom and Joe what I had tried
when all hell broke loose. That alarm clock finally went off.

Old Lucifer held true to form. He side-jumped
and kicked. By this time Slimtech had this move
down pat and he weathered the first part of the
storm pretty easy. But old Lucifer had had it. He
made up his mind that the lunch pail had to go,
and he started bucking like none of us had seen.
The only reason Slimtech rode 'im was cause
that mule kept bucking back under him. Tom
decided he better ride in and pick up that goofy

mule when the slicker came loose. The slicker hit Tom's horse in the face and that caused a minor wreck in itself.

While I was laughing at Tom old Lucifer and Slimtech passed us all in a one-mule stampede. All you could hear was a muffled alarm clock bell, a braying mule, and old Slimtech screaming something about revenge. I believe his exact words were "If I live through this I'll guarantee the fact that you won't." And with these immortal words drifting through the eastern New Mexico air, him and old Lucifer went out of sight into a shallow canyon.

Three or four days later a couple of cowboys rode into camp about supper time. They were pretty well up on news of the local area and they were free with all of their information. One little tidbit of news that gave me easier breathing was the story of how the schoolteacher finally made it to school one morning rather late. He looked terrible and was mumbling something about lynch mobs and vigilantes, outlawed kids, and goofy mules. Seems as though when old Lucifer finally quit running and Slimtech got off, he just unsaddled the mule and turned 'im loose. Then he walked back to town.

After he had calmed down enough to make any sense he quit talking. He turned in his resignation and started walking home. Rumor has it that he hired out as a piano player in a house of joy somewhere down around the border, where there wasn't any mules or alarm clocks, and no kids were allowed around.

A True Story about Cats: How Not to Get Rich Quick

BY CURT BRUMMETT

One spring day as Terry, Larry, and I, three schoolkids, were hanging around the pool hall on our lunch hour, we were discussing our financial crisis. We had just spent our allowances for the next 200 years replacing an outhouse that had disintegrated due to careless handling of four stolen sticks of dynamite, three blasting caps, one can of black powder and five gallons of kerosene. We didn't blow it up on purpose. But no one seemed to believe us.

After we got beat dang near to death we had to make arrangements to pay for the outhouse. It didn't matter that it hadn't been used in fifteen years. It had to be replaced. It wasn't our fault that lightning had hit our storehouse. And we never did figure out how they knew it was us that got the explosives. But the situation was we were dead broke and everybody in town was watching us like we had the plague.

We had decided that there was no way to get ahead money-wise, so we planned to learn how to play 42 for fun and profit.[22] We were watchin' ever so close when Elmo Carstead casually mentioned there were just too damn many cats around the store, the garage, and the pool hall. He also stated that if he killed 'em off the mice and rats would soon take over. So there he was, he just didn't know what he was going to do. Buell Addelman came up with the perfect solution:

"Elmo, that ain't no problem, all you got to do is castrate all the toms and that way you don't

lose any cats but you don't gain any cats either."
Buell never missed a play. Elmo came back by
stating he didn't have time to catch and castrate
those toms, 'cause when he wasn't waiting for
an important phone call he had to be at the pool
hall defending his championship. But the idea
was sure worth thinkin' on.

Buell bid 84 and mentioned that since everyone at the pool hall would benefit from such
good animal control, they could all chip in some
money and pay fifty cents per tom. That is if the
job was done right. Terry and I had done started
figuring. We guessed there must be sixty to
sixty-five toms out of that whole town full of
cats. Larry, being the only one showing any
sense, started slipping towards the door. Terry
got him stopped and started convincing him
about how easy it would be. After all, we had
helped castrate calves, colts, pigs, and sheep.
And besides, how else could three schoolkids
get rich quicker?

Terry was busy with Larry while I was busy
trying to get us hired on as custom cat cutters. It
took quite a bit of talking. Buell wasn't real sure
we had the experience to handle a job as important as this and Elmo wanted it done right. After
some pretty hard talking on my part Elmo and
Buell finally gave in and we sealed the deal.
Elmo said he would put out some scraps in an
old cement silo of his. Since it only had one
door, he could trap maybe thirty-five or forty
cats. The next day we could skip lunch and
come right over and make ten or fifteen dollars
right quick. He winked at Buell and the deal was
set.

We went on back to school and never said a word about our new money-making business. That night we all got our pocket knives sharpened to perfection. We knew that the sharper the knife the quicker the cut, and the quicker the cut, the more money we could make. The next morning at recess we got together and decided that a business of this importance deserved our full time attention. So we skipped out and headed for the pool hall. We found Elmo and Buell hard at work, keeping their championship, and convinced them that we wouldn't get in trouble for skipping class. After all, school was for kids too dumb to make any money. And besides, we already had our own business. We decided that after we cut all the local cats we might just go from town to town, as professionals.

Well, we followed Elmo and Buell out to that old silo and when they opened the door, I never saw so many cats in my life. It looked like there were a hundred in that room, and we guessed there must be at least half of 'em toms. Elmo and Buell were grinning. We thought they were happy 'cause they had found someone to do the job. Not so. Elmo said that part of the top of the silo was gone, and when he shut us in there would be plenty of light to see by. And when we got done cuttin' all those toms just holler and they would come and let us out.

When we stepped into that silo and they closed the door it dawned on all three of us that we didn't know beans about cuttin' cats. Now these cats were a long ways from being gentle housecats, and there probably weren't two in the whole place that had ever been touched by a human. But we didn't think about that, 'cause we were too busy listening to all that hissing and growling. You will never know what stark cold fear is until you are locked in a silo with a bunch of cats as scared as you are. We seriously discussed going back to school but we changed our minds on that, because if we went back failures we were sure to get in trouble. So we would just go ahead and get started.

Since I had the sharpest knife, it was decided that Terry and Larry would do the flanking. We started by Terry grabbing a big yellow tom. And from there things just went to hell. We figured that holding cats was probably like holding calves; once you get ahold of one, don't turn him loose. But we also discovered that turning a mad, scared cat loose wasn't all that easy. I didn't realize a cat could wreck so much stuff with two stout kids holding him. They got him stretched out and I cut him. Did you know that when you cut a scared cat that it changes their voice immediately and at the same time their kidneys go crazy? The sound from that cat made our hair stand on end, but all that water flying around made it lay back down. I announced that I was through with the surgery and they could turn 'im loose. I'll guarantee you one thing. Turning that cat loose took a lot longer than it did to catch him. Seemed like he was holding a grudge. Did you know a fresh castrated cat can scratch three kids (each one trying to escape) 96 times apiece while screaming and never draw a breath?

Now three kids trying to get away from a cat

in a silo is a pretty fair wreck, but trying to run away from one cat and stay away from 99 more (which by this time had gone as crazy as the one just cut) is disastrous. I don't know if it was Terry or Larry that ran through that door, but I'll love him forever. Relief comes in strange forms! When it was all said and done we gathered ourselves and took stock. There wasn't any place on any of us that didn't have a cat track of some kind on it. Not a one of us had a shirt left; they were just threads hanging around our necks and off our shoulders. When we finally calmed down a little, we looked back at the silo and there were cats still coming out that door.

We decided to call our folks instead of going back to school. The way we were hurting from those cat tracks, it wasn't going to make any difference who whipped us 'cause there was no way we were gonna hurt any more than we already were. We had a ton of explaining to our folks about the scratches and why we didn't have any shirts left and why we skipped school. Elmo and Buell not only had to explain to three mad moms, they had to give up their chairs in the pool hall for awhile. Seems a couple of mothers threatened to kill 'em if they were seen around town for awhile. Terry, Larry, and I didn't get a whipping. Our dads figured the cat tracks would be punishment enough. The next time Larry and Terry and I got together we decided that we would store our next batch of explosives behind the pool hall and hope for another electrical storm.

Come to think of it, we never got our fifty cents for cutting that cat.[23]

The sins men (and boys) do live after them, the poet says. After Curt published his account of the cat business in the *Livestock Weekly,* a year or two back, he swears the following consequences took place:

In Fantasy, Do-Gooders Don't Always Do So Good

BY CURT BRUMMETT

The other day I was confronted by two ladies from a Cat Club. At first I figured they were a couple of lost people. No one ever pulls up to our place except bill collectors or some misguided insurance salesman. Since I can spot a bill collector a quarter of a mile away, and they just didn't look like salesmen, I figured they were lost. Seems to me, the way I have figured in the past, I would've learned to give up figuring. As they stopped in front of the house, I left the horse I had been shoeing and walked over to say hello and see if I could help 'em out. I should've stayed with the horse.

The conversation went something like this:

"Yes ma'am, can I help you?"

"Are you Curt Brummett?"

"Yes'm. How much do I owe you?"

"Well, Mr. Brummett, you don't owe us anything but we believe you owe the animals you have abused and mistreated a great deal more than you could ever repay." Each word had enough venom dripping off it to supply all the rattlesnakes in eastern New Mexico and West Texas. I decided right quick I wouldn't invite 'em in for coffee. I've always been pretty hot-headed and prone to get myself whipped simply because I would blow smooth up and attack when I got mad. But I figured I would get in a lot more trouble from hitting this old bat in the eye than I would if I just let her rattle on. Besides that, this was my place and I could just tell 'em to leave.

"We are not here in any official capacity, we are just here to get an explanation for the way you seem to like to treat animals. Cats in particular, Mr. Brummett." She said this as she got out of her car. It was one of those foreign cars, and when she unloaded, the springs gave a sigh of relief as they came back to a semi-normal position. The other old gal started to get out too.

The first lady was about fifty to fifty-five and big. She had the coldest green eyes I had ever seen. She was wearing Levis and a khaki shirt. She was even wearing combat boots (actually, hiking boots). Her hair was kinda blood bay and fixed pretty nice. But she was big as me and moved like a tank. I wasn't scared, though; I still had my shoeing hammer in my hand. I figured if things got plumb out of hand I could always use it on myself to end all the pain this old gal looked like she could inflict on me. Her partner came around the front of the car. She looked like she could be twenty to thirty-five and stood about five-six. She was dressed about the same way as her friend and her hair was cut short. Now I'm not saying the woman was ugly, but if she was inclined to a military career she could have been a three-star general in the K-9 corps.[24] I gripped the hammer a little tighter.

They introduced themselves and then started demanding explanations. During all of this I was searching my brain trying to figure out what the hell they were talking about. I finally got 'em shut down and told 'em to talk one at a time and tell me just what it was I was supposed to have done that was so terrible. The big one, I'll call her Moose, took a step and pointed her finger. I raised the hammer a little.

"We heard about your cat castrating. Then when we came to talk to you about it, we had to ask directions how to get here. We stopped at the service station to ask where you lived, and-visited with two very nice men. They not only told us how to find your house, they explained how they have been trying for years to get you to give up your cruel ways. They even donated five dollars apiece to our organization and told us how good they thought we were for coming out here to try and get you to stop these terrible things."

Mike and H.L. were the first two to come to my mind. I chanced to look over my shoulder and sure 'nuff, there was Mike's pickup on top of the hill and I would've bet everything I owned they were sitting on the hood, each with a pair of field glasses and probably a cold beer. They're two sick people. I made up my mind that if I lived through this, I would get even.

I started to explain that I hadn't even touched a cat in twenty years, and that the only cat I ever cut lived to scratch hell out of three kids. And as far as being cruel to animals I would try to show them I wasn't. I would show them around my place and let them judge for themselves. After a quick tour of the horse pens, the chicken house, and speaking to each of the eight dogs, they calmed down considerably. Then it happened. Three pups and one big brown cat made their appearance, the pups in hot pursuit of the cat. Now one old brown cat had been hanging around my horse pens and haystacks for about two years. He sure helped keep the mouse problem under control and most of the birds out of the garden. But he always stayed out of sight. In fact, I hadn't even seen or thought of him in two or three weeks. But of course he had to pick today to show up.

I knew what he was gonna do and so did the older dogs. The only ones in the dark were the pups and those two goofy women. The lady general screamed, "We've got to help that poor kitty. Those mean dogs will chew her to pieces."

Moose Lady broke into a run to head off the dogs, and General headed for the poor kitty. Now the rest of them dogs figured if those two women could run that cat, they just might have a chance to whup it once and for all. And all eight dogs joined the chase. This particular cat was probably the toughest critter in all of eastern New Mexico and seven counties in West Texas. He weighed about twenty to twenty-five pounds, and had single-handedly whipped every dog that had ever showed up in our little town. His favorite trick was what he was trying to work this morning.

If he happened to be bored, he'd stroll around until he got the attention of some new pup or aggravate one of the older ones until he had an all-out chase going. He would run these pups all over the place, around the horse pens, the haystack and the roping chute, and then he would head for the middle of the arena. When he got

to his spot, he would turn and proceed to whup
hell out of whatever was chasing him. By the
time Moose and the General had got lined out,
the cat had made it to the arena. The only problem was this time when he turned around he
saw a little different situation. From his reaction,
I would say he wasn't really scared, just a little
confused. He not only had every dog on the
place coming for him, but he had a huge person
closing in on the dogs and a two-legged pit bull
closing in on him.

I know in my own mind he figured he could
handle the dogs, but the Moose and the General
were just too much to put up with. He sold out,
but just a hair too late. The General had cut
across and just as the cat turned the General
grabbed him. Yep, it was a terrible sight. And
the sounds weren't all that pretty either. The cat
proved what I had thought ever since he had
showed up. He didn't like to be handled.

When the General picked kitty up, she scared
him. The first thing kitty did was to put a lip
lock on the General's arm. This in turn caused a
scream similar to that of a gutshot werewolf.
The scream made the dogs think the cat was
hurt and could probably be whipped pretty easy,
so they attacked. The Moose thought the dogs
hurt the cat and she attacked. The General
knew the cat wasn't hurt, and all she wanted
was loose. Seemed from where I stood the General had had about all the rescue work she
wanted.

Now as most people know, when a cat feels
that his life is in danger, he climbs. It's his natural instinct. It doesn't make any difference what

it is, he's gonna climb. Well, this cat figured since he was already up off the ground, he might as well stay there. So he dug his old claws in and tried to ride the storm out. By now the General had developed an entirely different attitude concerning where that cat should be. She pulled him loose and gave him to Moose. This evidently pleased the cat because he climbed up Moose's pants leg, went up her back, and settled on her head. And I might add, this was no easy accomplishment.

For a large person, the Moose moved pretty good. She was kicking dogs, slapping at the cat, and using a strange language. By the time the cat reached the top of his new tree, I was right there and was fixing to start kicking dogs. Then the damnedest thing I ever saw happened. The General figured she had better help the Moose and waded right into the middle of the dogs. A brave move. She slapped that cat so hard she not only knocked the cat loose from the Moose but also knocked the wig plumb off the Moose's head. All you could see was two big old chunks of hair fly out over the dogs and hit the ground. Everything got quiet for about five seconds. I mean, all motion stopped. The dogs couldn't figure where that other cat had come from. The cat couldn't figure what kind of critter had chased it out of its makeshift tree. The General couldn't figure how she knocked the Moose's head off, and the Moose was trying to figure out why the General hit her instead of the dogs.

The cat was the first to move. He hauled freight and headed for the haystack. The dogs couldn't understand why the other cat just laid there, so they attacked. The two women looked at each other, started crying, and headed for the car. The Moose was a lot spookier-looking than she had been. I don't care how you look at it, a purt-near baldheaded woman that size is spooky. As they ran past me, I noticed neither one of them was hurt too bad. A couple of scratches and one or two fang marks, but nothing serious. Hell, I know for a fact, cat tracks will heal up.

By the time they had got in their car and left, things had calmed down considerably. The cat was on top of the haystack trying to figure out why that funny little furry critter wasn't putting up much of a fight. Mike and H.L. were rolling around on the ground, and I could hear them laughing from a quarter-mile away. The dogs had divided the wig equally and the pups were prancing around with their trophy. Each one figured they'd taught that cat a very important lesson.[25]

Pranks, whether the perpetrators are young or old, seem to be a vital part of cowboy humor. Some are wild (as the cowboy is supposed to be), and some are just good fun, but they help the cowboy pass the monotony of life with good cheer.

CHAPTER FOUR

The Ladies, God Bless 'Em

The West was not populated by cowboys alone. Obviously, there would not have been any little cowboys if there hadn't been some female counterparts for the family-oriented cattleman. In fact, several writers have gathered together impressive evidence of the vital roles played by the ladies in the West from earliest times on to the present. One scholar puts the matter quite clearly:

> How women on the cattle frontier took their place as equal partners with men is an important chapter in the history and folklore of the West. The cowboy may be our most authentic folk hero, but the cowgirl is right on his heels. Other types of frontier women passed with the

passing of the frontier and were more or less forgotten, but the cattlewomen, like the cowboys, found a way to stay in the saddle and survive. Until women make it aboard a rocket bound for the endless pastures of space, the cowgirl is likely to remain the American heroine.[1]

In support of this view, it is worth noting that Texas and the Southwest were settled especially by Southerners. Following the Civil War, when the former economic basis for life had come to an end, thousands of families went out to find new lives in the West. The Southern woman has long been celebrated in song and story for her strength and endurance. Many a family saga—from Southern clans such as my own—tells of how Grandma held the farm together while Grandpa was off in the Confederate Army. Stephen Vincent Benét hailed the ladies by example when he wrote of Mary Lou Wingate,

She was at work by candle light,
She was at work in the dead of night,
Smoothing out troubles and healing schisms
And doctoring phthisics and rheumatisms,
Guiding the cooking and watching the baking,
The sewing, the soap-and-candle-making,
The brewing, the darning, the lady-daughters,
The births and deaths in the negro-quarters, . . .
She was often mistaken, not often blind,
And she knew the whole duty of womankind,
To take the burden and have the power
And *seem* like the well-protected flower, . . .
And manage a gentleman's whole plantation

In the manner befitting your female station.[2]

Such a mixture of grace and ability, self-denial and toughness was sorely needed in early days in the West, a land of barren plains, dryness that withered the skin, wind that blew almost unceasingly, the absence of churches and schools and female company; then there was the frequent threat of Indians, with a host of tales circulating with graphic details of their barbarity. Women who lived in half-dugouts, as many did, could expect dirt and insects—some deadly—to fall into the food they cooked, and the rattlesnake's presence added its bit of excitement. "Frontier cattlemen were necessarily away from home much of the time," notes Joyce Roach, "and women found themselves with new responsibilities." Sometimes husbands deserted their families; sheer necessity soon taught women they had to pitch in if the ranch was to make a go of it. The gun, so often present in accounts of life in the West, was often quite deadly in the hands of a woman. One said she preferred the shotgun to the pistol, "because she could hit her victim over the head with it, back him up against a tree and poke his ribs with it, or she could pound his boot toe with it."[3]

Of course, like Mary Lou Wingate, the ranch woman was still a woman, usually the "helpmeet" of the man, and the raising of a family was her responsibility.

One mother, Mrs. Charlie Hart of New Mexico, who helped her husband herd cattle, solved her problem by taking it with her. She carried her first baby on the front of her saddle. When she had to make room on her saddle for a new baby, she tied the first child to the porch to prevent his falling into the well. Every two or three hours Mrs. Hart would ride back to the house to check on the child. When they reached the age of four, the children were mounted on their own horses and joined Mother on the range.[4]

Such a paragon of virtue and hard work as the Western woman hardly provides subject matter for humor. The woman, as has been noted earlier, was generally elevated to a point of reverence by the cowboy. But there were times when the individual woman did not live up to the ideal. Then it was that she provided laughter, but not often was the laughter smutty or demeaning. The closest to an off-color story involving women that I have come across deals with a rodeo performer who had an embarrassing problem in the arena. Deane Mansfield-Kelly, daughter of world champion calf-roper Toots Mansfield, tells me that wherever rodeo folks gather, the story of a certain cowgirl and her experience riding a saddle bronc is known and shared.[5] Joyce Roach tells the story as delicately as possible:

In the men's events, cowboys grabbed on to the pickup man's saddle or waist and jumped to the ground. A woman, because of the hobbles [a piece of leather tying the stirrups together under the horse's belly], required a pickup man's arm about her waist to steady her and assist her to safety. Needless to say, all the cowboys seemed available for the ladies' event and the cowgirls could pick and choose from among the best. The close contact provided some bawdy stories and moments of hilarity in the midst of real danger, as this story illustrates: One contes-

tant had reason to want off her horse in a hurry.
She had drawn a rough bucker and the animal's
violent landings caused her to hang her blouse
on the saddle horn. On the next trip skyward,
the cowgirl's blouse and underclothing were
ripped open. Her ample upper anatomy, now
unfettered, received a severe lashing along with
the rest of her body. Every time her head went
down, her bosom heaved upward. It was a few
minutes before the pickup could get to her, but
thinking of her embarrassment, he hurried.
When the man finally got there, her words were
not about her embarrassing predicament, but
rather, "For gosh sakes, somebody get me off
this horse before I black both my eyes."[6]

Another cowgirl on the rodeo circuit was involved in an
event that caused a lot of laughter—at least in the telling
and retelling. It has to do with a barrel-racer who is "a little
big" and rides a big, headstrong horse. After fighting the
horse to get him lined out in the alleyway leading to the
arena,

she's running. There was this guy just [acciden-
tally] walking across the end of the alley, where
the arena was. She hollered, "Look out!" and he
turned around and saw her coming. So he
throws his hands up and she hits him. He caught
his arm on the breast collar and she dragged
him all the way to the first barrel. You know
how most people would stop and be concerned.
Well, she beat him on the back with her crop all
the way to the first barrel because he was mess-

ing up her barrel run. Then, after it was over,
she went over and chewed him out.
I wasn't there at that. I just heard it. You
know, every time you hear about it, it gets more
exaggerated, depending on how much beer
you've had when you tell it. Like for instance, if
I'd had a little beer it could really turn into a big
story about how she beat him on every single
barrel, then roped his legs, tied him on, and
drug him across the pasture . . . .[7]

Maybe that barrel-racer was hard of heart, but rodeo cowgirls had to be tough of spirit as well. In one wild ride at
Madison Square Gardens, Ruth Roach came out second-
best to "a wicked devil-inspired bundle of steel muscles and
tough horse meat called Domino." She got up out of the
dirt—"only the dead stay down"—and went off to replace
the shirt that had been nearly torn from her body. She
came back smiling, but as a reporter wrote, "out there,
tramped into the stirred-up dirt where she went under the
thundering feet of Domino, lay a shining lock of golden
hair, sheared off her head as neatly as by a barber's scis-
sors, by those terrible flying hooves."[8]

The rodeo circuit had its jokers to relieve the boredom
between shows. The city dudes would come around, shining up to the cowgirls—usually to be given a quick brush-
off, because the men weren't rodeoers. One such, a very
rich man, loved to rodeo, but all he did was ride in the
grand entry before each performance, all dressed up in
white Western regalia and a huge peaked hat. The girls
picked a number out of the phone book, giving it to him as
from a fan who had seen him ride in the grand entry and
wanted him to come eat dinner with the family. "Lord
knows where it was in Boston. He got a taxi and went way

out there. He walks up to the door and those people had no more idea who he was! Oh, that was awful." Of course, such a trick was too good to keep, so it made the rounds. Tad Lucas thought she couldn't be caught by such a ruse, and for weeks nobody could trap her. But finally, one day she got a call from a man who said that he was the manager of Madison Square Gardens, and that she was needed over at Jack Dempsey's restaurant for publicity pictures with the champ. Naturally she got all gussied up, and hurried over with a girl friend. She had coffee, waited, and waited some more. Finally, after a good long while, she looked out the window at the sidewalk, "and here goes Harry Knight and Tom Johnson and Hub Whiteman, going by the window and peeking in! I thought, 'Well, they finally got me'."[9]

The ladies, rodeoers or just plain cow folks, still maintained their dignity and feminine standards. One rancher's widow who managed for herself and two children for several years had an experience that seems laughable today, but was deadly serious around the turn of the century. She had been driving a two-horse wagon out on the prairie when a horrendous rainstorm blew up. She took refuge under a tree, with a quilt draped over her head, but finally decided the horses were in danger from rising waters coming down a draw where she had tied them. Unhitching the team, she straddled one and was leading the other when a neighbor's boy, sent out to see about her, showed up. Well, she couldn't be seen riding astride, so she moved to a more ladylike position, sidesaddle with no saddle, atop her horse. He promptly stumbled and she slid off into muddy water, victim of her standards. The neighbor's boy laughed heartily, then showed her where the waters were less dangerous—but she rode sidesaddle the rest of the way despite her experience.[10]

Being a woman could cause complications on the ranch,

and the results were often comic—or at least, awkward. When Sid Skiver was trying to teach Maggie Howell the ins and outs of helping cows give birth, she appreciated his problem:

> He taught me a whole lot. We'd go out together and he had such an eye for everything. I'd say, "Sid, tell me a little more," and he'd start explaining some more things. I know he wanted to use the words that most of the guys use, like—oh, I don't know if I can say it [laughs], but words for the female anatomy—but he was always polite with me. He'd say, "Maggie, I want to just use these words but I can't quite say them to you. But you'll figure it out."[11]

On the ranch, the cowboys soon got used to the girls who worked alongside them, but other women were taboo. Amy Cooksley recalls an instance where she and her sister Elsie were just part of the crew:

> We were holding the herd one time while half the men had their dinner. We saw a lady and her daughter drive into the wagon for dinner. When the wagon came around, often the neighbors would come for a chuck wagon dinner. Our relief came out and told us we could go eat. One of the fellers that was helping hold the cattle said, "No way! I'm not going in there and eat with those women. I don't mind Amy and Elsie and the rest of the boys. But I'm not going in with those women."[12]

Apparently Amy was proud of being accepted as an equal by the cowboys, although she noted that they watched their language and didn't tell any dirty stories around her. But Maggie Howell felt differently:

> At first I was kind of on the bottom of the totem pole. I usually got all the old horses and the old harness—they didn't have anything else to give me. After I'd been here awhile, two fellas came up with two different workhorses. Another came driving in one day with a harness— not a new harness, but a nice one that wasn't all pieced together. . . . They were all sort of contributing to make it a little easier for me. . . . I feel very much at ease with the men I work around. I respect them and they respect me. I do my share of the work, they do theirs. And they'll still open a door for me, which is nice. I wouldn't want to be one of the boys.[13]

Toots Mansfield always said that his wife was the best cowhand he had, and another member of the family agreed. He told Deane Mansfield-Kelley, "Your mother was always there when she was needed. Now Annabelle [Deane's aunt] was always riding like hell to get there. But your mother was there already."[14]

Ranch work has attracted many women over the years. Melody Harper had a clear—and somewhat humorous— view of the importance of things in her own life: "To me, it's not enough to say, 'Well, gosh—I mopped the kitchen floor. I cleaned the closet. I did the washing and ironing.' I mean, so what?" And when she hired on as a ranch hand in Wyoming, she stipulated that she would not cook nor work in the yard; later on, when the boss let her break horses, she agreed to do the cooking, as long as the ranch work came first! But Melody is spurring hard for the nineteenth century; she even prefers a horse to a pickup. "Horses always start, they never run out of gas, they're never low on oil, you don't get greasy."[15]

As with the cowboy's life, humor sometimes comes unplanned and unexpected. A real-life incident on the Pitchfork Ranch involved an accident—and a lesson—to Tom, a cowboy whose manners were on the absent side, even when he ate at the ranch manager's table, with guests, ladies, and all. The manager's wife tells the tale:

> The actions of Tom's digestive organs were unpredictable, and uncontrollable, I suppose. He burped with noisy regularity, but sometimes I believed he gave especially impressive demonstrations for guests. "Where's the bakin' sody?" he'd ask loudly. Tom did everything loudly. Standing in plain view of us all, he'd gulp down an Arm and Hammer cocktail. Almost immediately, relief of room-rocking proportions would rumble forth. "Feel better'n I have in a long time," he'd say, fishing for the turkey quill from his pocket. He scorned the use of toothpicks that the cowboys reached for.
>
> Once when the dining room was filled with visitors, Tom made such a request, and in her haste, Mrs. Clary handed him the Twenty Mule Team Borax. Tom put a heaping teaspoonful in a glass of water, stirred vigorously, and polished it off at a single draught. We waited, fascinated, unbearably fascinated, for the reverberation, fork and knife suspended. It was impossible to

ignore. One could not go on talking, acting as if
nothing were about to happen, when you knew
that even the window panes might be shattered.
They almost were. Tom gave his prize performance. "Wups," he said, almost gently. "Wups!
What the hell?" Tom's burp rose to the occasion.
"*W-u-ps!*" And to our amazement and his, before
he reached the door, Tom was blowing bubbles
all over the place.[16]

Now despite the clear proof, offered herewith, that the
ladies, God bless 'em, make good hands on ranches, and
are often as good at doing "men's" jobs as the men are,
there comes the inevitable quibbler. Perhaps the quibble
arises from the fact that sometimes one of the ladies is not
"just one of the boys" after all, or maybe she's new at the
job. One lady—call her Mary—had married a rancher and
was anxious to help out. A bunch of cows was being run
through a gate into a small pasture, away from the prize
bull the rancher doted on. Mary was to stay out of the way
and be a good girl. But her horse looked hungry, so she
opened the gate into the pasture and let him through—just
about the time the bull got wind of the females nearby. He
came at a trot, headed for the gate where Mary stood.
Mary got the picture, and swiftly—too swiftly—pulled the
barbed wire gate shut in front of the now charging bull.
Mary was proud of herself, having been so alert. Then she
was astounded to hear her husband shout, "Open the
gate!"

The wife was even more astounded when she
looked up just in time to see the bull run right
over the gate, leaving his bullish credentials

93

impaled on the barbed wire. The new steer proceeded to his appointed rounds which neither
rain, nor snow, nor dark of night, nor lack of
wherewithal could stay.[17]

The loss of a ten-thousand-dollar bull had a dampening
effect on the couple's relationship, one might suppose. The
former bull probably wasn't too happy about it either.

Another event—not quite so permanent—involved a
cowhand's wife who was asked to help out with vaccina-
tion duties, because the foreman was short-handed. The
heifers were to be inoculated with Abortus (to reduce their
tendency to lose their calves), and both heifers and steers
were to receive Black Leg serum.

The lady was hard at work, shooting with two needles
and not noticing what the cowboys were up to, when the
foreman announced, "That's all the steers. Now let's get the
heifers." Suddenly the lady realized that she had made a
slight error. But she was equal to the occasion when her
husband exploded, asking her what she had to say for
herself.

"Well," she replied with her head down. "When I get
done, ain't no steers goin' to lose no calves, and ain't no
heifers gonna get Black Leg in this herd."[18]

When you can't get good help, you have to make do with
what you can get, I reckon, but Curt Brummett goes to
great extremes to avoid asking his wife for help. If the
following story is true, then perhaps he has reason.[19]

Good Help Is So Hard to Find
BY CURT BRUMMETT

I have heard that windmills can be fun. And
I'm sure, or at least pretty sure, that it can be if

you are the windmiller, and not the windmillee.
I have on occasion had the pleasure of being the
windmiller instead of the windmillee, but not
very often. Of course you know the difference,
but for those that don't, I'll explain. The windmillee is the poor slob that gets to help the
windmiller.

The windmillee can be any shape, size and
purt near any age. And they can be of either
sex. But female windmillees are used only as a
last resort. By this I mean the windmiller has
had to have gone through every neighbor, every
wetback, tried to clean out the bars for winos,
and even tried to trick an innocent tourist before he resorts to having a female-type windmillee help 'im out. And of course the female I'm
talking about is the Little Woman.

Now on the few times I'd have the privilege to
be the windmiller, I've only had to use a female-
type windmillee twice. Actually both times were
the same, my first and my last. All the other
times I managed to trap a neighbor or find some
unsuspecting compadre coming out of the local
tavern, after a bit too much of the bubbly. However, them bubbly-type buddies have a tendency
to want to take naps. Especially if they started
sucking on the suds very early in the day. I once
conned two wetbacks into helping me, but due
to rather informal tools, and a complete lack of
Spanish, I lost 'em.

Once just before the Fourth of July rodeo, I
had a set of leathers go bad in a well in the west
pasture. Normally I would have just moved
some cattle around and fixed them after the
roping. But I had just put some straightened-out

yearlings in there and I needed all the fresh water I could get.

Since all the neighbors were tied up with their own problems, or already gone to some of the rodeos scattered around the country, I figured that me and the little woman could pull the rods and have the well pumping by late afternoon. I mean, it was only the second and I wasn't up in the steer roping until the afternoon of the third. With the little woman helping me, I had plenty of time. Everything but the time element was bad figuring.

Now let me say this about the little woman. She is probably the best cook west of the Mississippi, and she can make a shirt better than any professional tailor. And at times she can have the sweetest disposition in the world. But at times she can get plumb snarly. And in spite of all the good things I can say about her, I feel like I should tell you this: she don't take orders worth a damn, and she sure as hell don't take constructive criticism. Any hoo—after I rode back to the house, and got the tools loaded in the pickup, I finally convinced her to come help me.

Since it was a shallow well, I figured I could pull it by hand and all she would have to do would be to set the wrenches. (I figured this out because my neighbor Jason Outagear had borrowed all my windmill tools. Pretty sharp figuring!) Well, I finally got the little woman and old Jughead (my pit bull queensland heeler cross-bred cowdog pup) loaded. Since we only had to go through eight gates, I let her drive. Mainly because her and that goofy pup had never learned to shut a gate properly.

It was about 11:30 in the morning when we finally got to the well. Jughead jumped out of the pickup and laid down in the shade. Yep, that dog was showing more and more sense all the time. After I got everything loose and ready to go, I adjusted the wrenches and explained to her what I wanted her to do. I got started pulling on the rods, and by the time I finally got the check out of the cylinder, I thought my hemorrhoids had hemorrhoids. I got to the first coupling and told her to put the wrench on the bottom rod, and pull up on the handle. I set the weight of the rods on the wrench, let the wrench rest on the top of the pipe, broke the top rod loose, and stood it in the corner of the tower. As smooth as it went, I thought to myself, "Self, this may go a lot better than I figured."

That was about the only good thought I had for the rest of the day.

Two rods later, Jughead figured he would get into the act. He came charging into the tower and jumped on the little woman's leg so he could get a better look. He not only got a better look, he scared hell out of the little woman. She screamed, spooked me, and I dropped the rods that were still in the well. I heard 'em hit bottom. I commented on the fact that Jughead was really something to be scared of. After all, he was all of eight months old, and had been known on occasion to maul hell out of a warm buttered biscuit.

She mentioned that since I was so big and bad and brave, and always had total control, I could run the first rods back down the well and fish the others out. (Me being the type never to mouth off, I didn't tell her what I would like to do with those rods.) I started wondering if there might be any tourists at the coffee shop in town. It was about 12:30.

Well, I run the rest of the rods in, got tied on to the ones I'd dropped, and started pulling 'em out again. By now we had a pretty good audience. About two hundred steers, thirty antelope, and a double handful of jackrabbits. I put Jughead in the back of the pickup to avoid a major wreck with the steers. You know how aggressive a cowdog pup can be. I unseated the top check again, and this time we had all but three rods out. The little woman happened to look around and see the antelope.

I wouldn't have minded her taking time out to appreciate the local wildlife, but she happened to notice the critters at the same time I thought she had hooked the rods. Have you ever heard three rods speeding to the bottom of a 180-foot well? They didn't make near the noise I did. I kinda raised my voice a little. The antelope ran off, and the steers spooked a little. When the steers spooked, Jughead woke up.

I casually mentioned to the little woman that she had better keep her mind on her work, or things could get a little rough. When I finally got her to put the wrench down, I climbed down off the platform and started running rods back into the well. It was about 1:45.

There is an old saying, the third time's the charm. This time it held true. We finally got all the rods out, the new blackjacks on, and all the rods back in the well. I think the reason we got

along so good on this trip was we were so mad
we didn't hardly say anything. But as I was starting to hook up the red rod, things got plumb out
of hand. During the run back to the bottom, the
steers got to thinking they needed a closer look
at what was going on. They had eased up to and
all around the windmill tower, just to watch the
little woman and myself struggle to get them
water. While they was watching us, Jughead was
watching them. I watched my steps, and the
little woman was watching for more antelope.
One steer had noticed Jughead, and that's all it
took. It was about 3:15.

When Jughead bit that steer on the end of the
nose, he forgot to turn loose. It was the pit bull
in him. Now one steer running backwards with
a dog on the end of his nose is pretty spooky to
the other 199 that's been standing around mind-
ing their own business. Especially if the dog's
growling, the steer's bellowing, and the little
woman's screaming. When about half the steers
bumped the tower, I fell off the guide boards.
About the time I hit the ground, the little
woman bailed off into the stock tank. Jughead
and the steer broke through the bottom brace
on the tower and came inside with me.

I don't care what anyone says, it only takes
one steer, one dog, and one mad woman to
have a stampede in a six-by-six-foot pasture.
Somewhere between the third and eighty-sec-
ond pass over my back and head, I grabbed Jughead's legs and purt near ripped the steer's lips
off. When the steer got rid of all that unwanted
weight and pain, he paused for just a second.
When he saw me and the furry little critter that

bit 'im, he turned and joined the little woman in the water tank. Of course, the little woman was in the process of coming back to the surface, and she didn't see her swimming companion take the dive.

That crossbred steer hit the little woman right square in the hip pockets. Contrary to popular belief, a woman can skip across water just like a flat rock. I didn't know what to do first, kill that damned dog or help the little woman out of the water tank. It took only a couple of minutes— seconds, really—to make a decision. I turned the dog loose and ran. I could tell she wasn't hurt by the way she was chasing Jughead and swinging that wrench. I told her if she would just calm down, I would drive her to the house. She informed me she didn't want to calm down, and she could drive herself to the house.

What was the last straw, she got in the pickup and started to leave, and that traitor of a dog jumped in the back just as she was starting to pull out. That dog wasn't a complete dummy. As they was going out of sight, I turned the windmill on and gathered up what tools I could find. I stacked them inside the tower, and then I started walking home.

It wasn't that bad, 'cause this way I could still make the roping, and know for sure that all the gates was shut properly. It was about fifteen till four.[20]

I reckon, until all the votes are in, I'll have to go with the bulk of the evidence. Seems that the ladies, God bless 'em, are generally pretty handy to have around the ranch. I think ole Curt was just snakebit. And he might consider giving Jughead to a friend—or an enemy even, one who's lacking excitement in his life.

CHAPTER FIVE

Cosi—The Cowboy's Cook

The trail drive of the American cowboy is well known to the reading and viewing public of the entire world, thanks to the influence of television and movies and their enormous capacity for education. As is also well known, unfortunately Hollywood is not always careful with its facts—indeed, a new folklore might well be said to have developed because of the public media's role in passing on information and misinformation. Such is the nature of oral transmission itself, of course: in the case of the "Old West" one old cowpoke remembers singing to the cattle to keep them calm; another points out that the average cowboy's voice was far from soothing, and his songs might well have precipitated (rather than averted) a stampede. Of course, with the dulcet tones of Gene Autry and the Sons of the Pioneers as evidence, the popular view is of the romantic persuasion, as is much of the lore of the American cowboy.

Usually overlooked are the factual matters of the cowboy cook and his rolling kitchen. Of course, "everybody" knows that chuck wagon cooks are genially irascible—"as techy as a chuck wagon cook," goes the old saying.[1] George "Gabby" Hayes of the Western movies of the 1940s is an excellent example; and all Western movie buffs know that a chuck wagon looks pretty much like an ordinary covered wagon with a pregnant tailgate. But that's about as much as most folks know. The day-to-day routine of the cook gets him up hours before breakfast to rustle grub for a bunch of unruly, and often unappreciative, cowpokes. Then there is the day-long battle to keep ahead of the herd, arriving at designated meal-stops with enough time to spare to put together a meal that would stick to the ribs. But all that is a largely unsung epic.

The portions that have been sung are all part of the past, recorded reminiscences of cowboys and bean-artists who have long since gone up the Long Trail. Still, from those memories a pretty clear picture can be drawn of the lore of the chuck wagon cook. Frank S. Hastings, veteran manager of the SMS ranch, wrote that

> a Ranch in its entirety is known as an "Outfit,"
> and yet in a general way the word "Outfit" sug-
> gests the wagon outfit, which does the cow-
> work and lives in the open from April 15th,
> when the work begins, to December 1st, when it
> ends.[2]

Thus for three-quarters of a year the chuck wagon was home for a dozen or so cowpunchers, and the cook was the center thereof. The cowhands stuck pretty close to camp:

They rarely leave the wagon at night, and as the
result of close association an interchange of wit
or "josh" has sprung up. There is nothing like
the chuck wagon josh in any other phase of life,
and it is almost impossible to describe. . . . It is
very funny, very keen, and very direct.[3]

This "josh" Hastings wrote of is the very heart of the family
feeling that cowboys had on roundup or on the trail. There
they ate their beans and beef, drank coffee—usually Arbuckles' brand; around the cook's fire they rested, swapped
yarns and songs, and slept when they could. The chuck
wagon was home for much of the time. And even though
the movies have given some glimpses of the chuck wagon
and its majordomo, perhaps it would be worth the effort to
give a real-life picture from one who knew the whole
matter firsthand.

Jack Thorp, Easterner-turned-cowboy who wrote *Songs
of the Cowboys,* among other works, described "A Chuck
Wagon Supper" for the New Mexico Federal Writers Project of WPA days. Apparently he never published this clear
picture of a bygone scene:

A chuck wagon arrives at Milagro Springs.
The cook, who has been driving, hollers "Whoa,
mule," to the team of four which has been pulling the load. Getting off the seat he throws
down the lines, and calls to the horse wrangler,
who is with the remuda of saddle horses following the wagon, to "gobble them up," meaning to
unhitch the team and turn them into the remuda.

The cook now digs a pit behind the chuck

105

wagon, so when a fire is built, the wind will not blow sparks over the camp and the punchers surrounding it. The chuck wagon is always stopped with the wagon tongue facing the wind; this is done so that the fire will be protected by wagon and chuck box. The wrangler, with rope down, drags wood for the fire. The many rolls of bedding are thrown off the wagon, and the cook brings forth his irons. Two of them are some four feet long, sharpened at one end, and with an eye at the other end. The third is a half-inch bar of iron some six feet long. Once he has driven the two sharpened irons into the ground above the pit, the long iron is slipped through the eyes of the two iron uprights; this completes the pot-rack, or stove. Cosi, as the cook is usually called—which is an abbreviation of the Spanish word *cocinero*—hangs a half-dozen or so S-hooks of iron, some six inches long, on the suspended bar, and to these are hooked coffee-pot, stew pots, and kettles for hot water.

The rear end of the wagon contains the chuck box, which is securely fastened to the wagon box proper. The chuck box cover, or lid, swings down on hinges, making a table for Cosi to mix his bread and cut his meat upon, and make anything which may suit his fancy. . . . There is an unwritten law that no cow puncher may ride his horse on the windward side of the chuck box or fire, or Cosi is liable to run him off with pot-hook or axe. This breach of manners would be committed only by some green hand, or "cotton-picker," as Cosi would call him. This rule is made so no trash or dirt will be stirred up and blown into the skillets.

The cocinero, now having his fire built, with a pot-hook in hand—an iron rod some three feet long with a hook bent in its end—lifts the heavy Dutch bake oven lid by its loop and places it on the fire, then the oven itself, and places it on top of the lid to heat. These ovens are skillets about eight inches in depth and some two feet across, generally, but they come in all sizes, being used for baking bread and cooking meat, stew, potatoes, and so forth. The coffeepot is of galvanized iron, holding from three to five gallons, and hanging on the pot rack full of hot coffee for whoever may pass. Then Cosi, in a huge bread pan, begins to mix his dough. After filling his pan about half-full with flour, he adds sour dough, poured out of a jar or tin bucket which is always carried along, adds salt, soda, and lard or warm grease, working all together into a dough, which presently will become second-story biscuits. After the dough has been kneaded, he covers it over, and for a few minutes lets it "raise."

A quarter of a beef is taken from the wagon, where it has been wrapped in canvas to keep it cool. Slices are cut off and placed in one of the Dutch ovens, into which grease—preferably tallow—has been put. The lid is laid on, and with a shovel red hot coals are placed on top. While this is cooking, another skillet is filled with sliced potatoes, and given the same treatment as the meat.

Now the bread is molded into biscuits, and put into another Dutch oven. These biscuits are softer than those made with baking powder, and as each is patted out, it is dropped into hot grease and turned over. These biscuits are then put in the bake oven, tight together until the bottom of the container is full. Now comes the success or failure of the operation. The secret is to keep the Dutch oven at just the right heat, adding or taking off the right amount of hot coals, from underneath the oven or on top of the lid. If everything goes right, you may be assured of the best hot biscuits in the world.

Sometimes a pudding is made of dried bread, raisins, sugar, water, and a little grease, also nutmeg and spices. This is the usual cow-camp meal, but if there is no beef in the wagon, beans and chili are substituted.[4]

When researching the lore of the chuck wagon cook, I wondered how Cosi managed to cook *frijoles* (pinto beans) when he and the wagon were on the move so much of the time. Beans generally require several hours to cook. Buck Kelton finally revealed the system: Cosi put the beans on to soak after supper, then put them on the fire first thing in the morning, or even at bedtime the night before. When he broke camp, he put the lid on the pot, which was hung still boiling in the chuck wagon, where they continued to cook for quite a while. When he reached the spot chosen for dinner—the midday meal—they went back on the fire. By the time the rest of the meal was ready, so were the beans—the best you ever hooked a lip over![5] Considering the difficulty of cooking three meals a day for a bunch of men, and the concentration and work involved, it is quite understandable that the cook earned a reputation for being "techy." And the chuck wagon "josh," while it was generally spread around among all the men, was quite often aimed at the "'gut robber,' 'dough-boxer,'

'Sallie,' 'greasy belly,' 'bean-master,' 'belly-cheater,' or 'biscuit shooter'."[6] The cook's little world was sacred, off limits to the loafer; in fact, one report has it that the cook usually threw his dirty dishwater under the chuck wagon: "The practice was designed to discourage drowsy cowhands from sneaking under the wagon for a nap in the shade, and protected the cook's hallowed domain."[7]

Of course, to tease the cook, cowboys often played at violating that sacrosanct territory—sometimes with results that were not funny at all. A cowboy named Hinton once pushed his luck too far with a chuck wagon cook known as Frenchy,

> digging into the chuck box, which was against Frenchy's rule, as it was with any good cooky. They did not want the waddies messing up the chuck box. Hinton seemed to get a kick out of seeing French get riled. . . . Frenchy never refused to give anyone a handout, but Hinton insisted upon helping himself. The evening that the fight took place, Hinton walked past Frenchy and dove into the chuck box. Frenchy went after Hinton with a carving-knife and Hinton drew his gun. The cooky kept going into Hinton slashing with his knife and Hinton kept backing away shooting all the while, trying to get away from the knife, but Frenchy never hesitated . . . ; finally he drove the knife into Hinton's breast and they both went to the ground and died a few minutes later.[8]

Most teasing, of course, did not go that far. Sometimes, however, a bad cook, or one the law was after, or one who caught more than what he considered his share of the "josh," would ask for his time and leave the outfit without a cook. This situation set up one of the most widespread of chuck wagon cook jokes, that of the substitute cook. Usually, as described in my introduction, when something happened to the cook a make-do got stuck with the job, to serve till somebody complained. Not out of basic politeness nor consideration for the substitute cook, but out of a dislike for the job, nobody complained. The replacement, as Philip Rollins points out, was just a cowboy with no training for the unwanted task of feeding the hands, washing dishes, and so on. One cowboy saved his own hide, after having exploded—"This bread is all burned, but gosh! that's the way I like it." In another version of the story, the problem was biscuits: "They are burnt on the bottom and top and raw in the middle and salty as hell, but shore fine, just the way I like 'em."[9]

Both the tradition of using substitute cooks and a host of stories arising out of the situation are mentioned in *Come and Get It*, and I've often been told the same tale—with the difference that the beans have an added ingredient, usually cow manure. This detail links the story with a Maine lumberjack story with the same theme: the unwilling cook served up a dish that should have gotten him fired. Both a tale and a ballad came out of the supposed event, with the conclusion of the ballad speaking for itself:

> One by one the boys turned green,
> Their eyeballs rolled to and fro;
> Then one guy hollered as he sank to the floor,
> "My God, that's moose-turd pie!
> [Shouted] Good though!"[10]

110

Lest Frenchy, who resented Hinton's invasion of his territory, go to his reward with a bad name, it is worth pointing out that there was another side to him. A cowpoke named John Baker tells the story:

The belly-cheater on the Holt outfit was a fellow called Frenchy, a top cooky. He was one of them fellows that took enjoyment out of satisfying the waddies' tapeworm. Frenchy was always pulling some tricks on us waddies and we enjoyed his tricks, because he always made up for the tricks by extra efforts in cooking some dish we hankered after. He could make some of the best puddings I ever shoved into my mouth. One day at supper we were all about done eating and Frenchy said: "If you damn skunks wait a second I'll give you some pudding. It is a little late getting done." Of course we all waited and he pulled a beauty out of the oven. We all dived into it and took big gobs into our mouths. We then started to make funny faces. What he had done was to use salt instead of sugar when he made it and that pudding tasted like hell. We all began to splutter and spit to clean out our mouths. He then pulled a good pudding on us and that sure was a peach. We had forgot that the day was April 1. He would use red pepper in some dishes we hankered after, also cotton in biscuits, but we knew something extra was coming up to follow.[11]

Another cook—a substitute this time—pulled a stunt that is worth repeating. There was to be a dance nearby, and

Stub Rutter had drawn the short straw after the regular cook hurt his leg and had to be hauled off to the doctor. Stub was a good cook, but the boys were joshing him about he was gonna be a couple hours late to the dance, because of washing up after supper and all. He never paid 'em any mind, and served up

beef and a couple of skillets of fried potatoes that come out of the oven smellin' good enough to make any camp cook proud. The boys dug into them like they'd never seen fried potatoes before. They ate 'em up so fast nobody noticed that Stub was cut out of his share.

Supper over, every hand spruced up and hit leather for the dance, all a-hootin' something smart at Stub, busy washing dishes.

At the dance, though, the girls didn't seem none too sociable. They'd dance with a fellah once and from then on a polite shake of the head with a cold stare was all a hand would rate. Every hand of the outfit reached the wall-flower stage when Stub finally came in on the scene. The fellahs all stood around waitin' to josh Stub when he'd get turned down like the rest of us. Only thing was, things didn't work out that way. Stub danced every darn dance, while the rest of us couldn't beg a partner.

It wasn't till the boss showed up on the scene that we began to figure the trouble.

"What in hell you fellahs been eatin'?" the old man roared at a couple of us when we come along side of him to find out how the injured cook was makin' out. "All of you stink like so much buzzard bait."

After Stub had been coaxed with a few head duckin's in the waterin' trough, he finally up and confessed. Cook had carried some garlic in his mess board to use in the beef, case we had to go for some fresh-kill stuff. Stub had put all the garlic in our fried potatoes and scented us up like so many pole-cats. He said he was afraid we'd have all the girls for the dances before he could get there, so he played safe. He was darn careful not to go for them garlic potatoes himself.[12]

And even a regular cook like old Sour-face Smith could make a mistake from time to time—but nobody dared to kick about it.

I remember one time old Sour-face was fixin' up a mess of beans for the outfit and somehow a bar of soap got in the bean pot. I guess Sour-face saw the soap all right when he was stirrin' the mess up but he thought it was a hunk of lard or some bacon rind he had thrown in with the mess. Anyway, about the first hand that grabbed a mouthful of them beans let a howl out of him and started spittin' them out. Old Sour-face came chargin' in. "What's the matter with them beans?" he roars.

That howlin' hand was an old range head and he was readin' the battle in Sour-face's eyes. "Not a damn thing, Sour-face," he come back, quick-like. "It's my tooth. The one you put turpentine in yesterday. It's jumpin' like a kickin' colt."

We all ate them beans, soap and all after that

remark. Sour-face might've found out the trouble later but he never said nothin'. Only thing was, we had pie and puddin' every day for the next week. If Sour-face did taste his own mess of beans he sure appreciated the crew's loyalty enough to try to make up for his mistake.[13]

Rather than his essential beans and beef—and even an occasional pie or cobbler—the cook was judged by his coffee. "Around chuck wagons," says Francis Fugate, "early Westerners renewed their energies with coffee, the aromatic brew that 'quickens the spirit and makes the heart lightsome.' Chances are that Arbuckles' was the brand in all those coffeepots. In fact, the use of Arbuckle Bros. coffee was so widespread that its brand name became synonymous with the word 'coffee'. . . ."[14] The cook, strongly supported by the cowhands, believed in making it stout: "A recipe went the rounds from ranch to ranch, confided by cooks to greenhorn hands: 'You take two pounds of Arbuckles', put in enough water to wet it down, then you boil it for two hours. After that, you throw in a horseshoe. If the shoe sinks, the coffee ain't ready.'"[15]

The cook was vital to a happy outfit, and his welfare—if he was a good bean-shooter—gave him special privileges. Philip Rollins says that if somebody ragged the cook too much, he could be required to serve for twenty-four hours as an assistant or even as substitute.[16] Although there are stories of the outfit where the cowboys were fed so poorly it took three of them standing sideways to cast a shadow,[17] probably more typical was old Sour-face, a good cook who kept the hands from quitting once on a roundup. The Holy 7 boss had been riding the boys hard, and the rough steers they'd been gathering up were rambunctious, so they got together and decided they'd all quit, right after supper.

Well, Sour-face told 'em they were quitters, and that he and the chuck wagon were staying on.

When the crew rode in for supper, they started smelling pies—and, sure enough, there were a dozen brown-crusted pies cooling on the tailgate of the wagon, with the Holy 7 brand cut in the lid of each one. They were looking forward to a good dessert before leaving, but Sour-face told 'em, "Stay 'way from those pies, you lop-eared galoots, them's for breakfast." Nobody could have talked a one of 'em into leaving that night, and with the pie for breakfast they were full of brotherly love—and nobody had any thought of quitting.[18]

Sometimes an amateur would try his hand at cooking, like the rookie Texas Ranger who decided he'd help out by cooking a week's worth of rice for his squad. The rice started off all right, but then it began to swell. He divided it up into two kettles, but they were soon overflowing too, so he dipped and he dipped and he dipped, and finally he had to pour a lot of it out on the ground—and even then he had enough rice to feed the whole company.[19]

That oversupply of rice recalls stories of cooks who fed too much of the same thing, sometimes because the owner was cheap and didn't take too much stock in pampering the hands. For beef-loving cowboys, too much salt pork was a major cause for complaint: "We was fed so much sowbelly we sweated straight lard."[20] One crew didn't like the "too solid" chuck set before them; "once when they bellyached for something fancy he took nothing but canned peaches on a ten-day trial trip. The last two days out the boys eat three badgers, a armadillo, and two coyotes."[21]

Buck Kelton, longtime manager of the McElroy Ranch of Crane, Texas, as a boy was in a bunch of cowboys whose boss had a habit of buying up damaged freight to feed his hands—especially dented gallon cans of molasses. Now a good cook could do wonders with limited materials, but the M Ranch man "wasn't no cook, he was a farmer." And a steady diet of molasses for sweetening with no variety got a little old. His tomatoes and corn with little or no beef got tiresome too. Buck was sent to town with a wagon to load up some of those damaged goods, including four or five cardboard boxes, each with six gallon cans of syrup. He wasn't too happy about seeing all that molasses.

> Waitin' for the cook to get ready to leave, me'n old Billy Pease were laying there in the shade of the wagon, and noticed that you could see the boxes through the cracks in the wagon bed, about a quarter of an inch wide. And old Billy said, "Reckon we can reach up there with our pocket knives and puncture those sons a bitches?" I stuck my pocket knife up there and I reckon I punched about four or five of those cans, and all the way out to the M Ranch we could see the syrup a stringin' down. Time we got to the ranch they were over half empty, and me and Billy was laughing at all that syrup spilling out.[22]

Sometimes it wasn't a cook's work but his nature that cost him his job. Nora Ramírez's father recalls from childhood a cook who didn't last long:

> One day we went to the Grapevine Horsecamp and they had about twenty to twenty-five men with the chuckwagon and they put me back in the corner to eat. When everybody got coffee (I

was just a little kid, seven years old) I never
thought about gettin' me a cup of water and I
got in there and finally, about to choke down, I
asked that cook if he wouldn't mind gettin' me a
drink of water and he asked me when did he get
to be my servant and give me a pretty good
talkin' to; so I asked 'em all to get up and let me
get the water. By God, they all got up and let me
go get my cup of water and whenever the meal
was over and everythin' done why Lee [the
boss] told that cook, "You can roll your beddin'.
When anybody can't be no nicer to a kid than
that, why he don't need to be here."[23]

Long rides away from the chuck wagon, or days spent
trying to round up cattle scattered in a stampede, sometimes made a cowboy go without food longer than was
comfortable—but he took it with a grin. On one such
occasion, a cowboy a long ways from home came to a
river: "The water was good and I took a 'Spanish supper'—
tightened my belt up a notch. . . . I slept very little. About
daybreak I rode back to the river and had plenty of water
for breakfast." After a time he came to a house, and asked
to buy some corn for his horse. The lady told him to take
all he needed, without pay, and asked if he had had breakfast. "Yes," he replied, with typical cowboy understatement, "I drank some coffee about three o'clock in the
morning at Tascosa two or three days ago." He stayed for
breakfast.[24]

Some stories about food and cooks strain the faith of the
most credulous. Mody Boatright tells of a Texas Ranger and
a camp cook who have to prepare dinner with no fuel—not
even any buffalo chips or cow chips—but the prairie grass
is dry and tall. The grass is set on fire, and as the fire moves

with the wind, the Ranger follows it with his steak wrapped about a ramrod, while the cook hurries along with pots and pans, cooking on the run. When the meal is finally done the pair find they are eight miles from camp.[25]

A fabulous cowboy and cook named Pie-Biter has had a number of stories circulated about him (including the above one). His name came about from his eating habits:

> He was very fond of sweet potato pie and would consume several pies at one sitting. His favorite manner of eating them was to stack them one above the other and bite through them all at once. From biting through two pies at a time, he advanced with practice to biting through three at once. Like most talented persons, he strove to perfect himself and before long was biting through four pies. . . . Then came a day when he felt the urge to bite through five pies. He made known his ambition, and there was a great gathering of the yeomanry to see him make the attempt. Someone bet him he could not perform the feat. He at once accepted and the money was put up.
>
> In the presence of a great multitude he stepped bravely forward for the test. The pies were stacked before him, one, two, three, four, five. Women wept and strong men shuddered as the moment drew near. When Pie-Biter, opening his cavernous mouth to its fullest reach, encompassed with his jaws all five of the pies, a mighty cheer arose from the throng. Suddenly a look of dismay and then of anguish spread over Pie-Biter's features and his teeth sank inexorably into the pie. He could not make his teeth meet.

Try as he might, he was unable to bite through the stacked pastry.

In a moment he abandoned the attempt, bursting into the bitter scalding tears of disappointment. And not until then did he discover that somebody had failed to remove the tin plate from under one of the pies.[26]

A variation on the substitute cook theme occurs in one of Curt Brummett's stories, in which Curt is sent out to a camp to work with another waddie collecting strays missed in the roundup. Curt was to do dishes, while Carlton, the other man, did the cooking. Carlton said that the first to gripe would be stuck with both jobs. As Curt recalls, "I should have suspected something at that statement but being the dumb kid I just ignored it. That was one mistake I will never make again." The meals got progressively worse, but Curt didn't complain. His story continues:

Good Groceries and Clean Dishes
BY CURT BRUMMETT

After a week of eating beans that rattled like bullets when they hit the plate, and bacon that either slid off the plate and squealed as it ran out the door, or shattered into a million pieces when you touched it with a fork, I was purt near ready to start cooking. But not quite.. Then one morning after breakfast, I made up my mind. Something had to be done. I mean, when a man hands you a plate of bacon, eggs, biscuits and gravy, and the only thing you recognize is the plate, it's time to do something.

But I kept quiet, chipped myself out a cup of

coffee, and tried to eat. It has been said that a hungry man will eat purt near anything, but this is not always true. I know, because I was damned sure hungry, and I left a bunch of that stuff on my plate. It is extremely difficult to eat eggs that cackle when you cut them. And I have yet to figure out how he burned just half of each piece of bacon and left the other half raw. The biscuits were so gooey you could have used them for caulking compound, and had enough salt in them that they weighed two pounds apiece. The gravy wasn't all that bad. I just cut it up into bite-sized squares, and put 'em in my pocket. I figured I could chew on 'em while I was ridin' pasture.

When I finished washing the dishes and started to go catch my horse, old Carlton mentioned the fact that I didn't eat much breakfast. Since I had just finished washing and stacking all the dishes, I didn't throw anything at him. I just smiled and told 'im that all those good groceries was startin' to put weight on me, and I had just made up my mind to start watching my waistline. He just smiled, said, "Anytime you want to do the cooking, you can sure have it. But since I enjoy it so much, I hope you won't take it away from me." The man was sure pushing his luck.

As we rode out that morning, my mind was working in high gear. I just couldn't figure this man out. I had been working with Carlton for eight days and I still didn't know his last name. Unless it was a have-to case, there was little or no conversation. And there was no way I could figure out why he so cheerfully destroyed good groceries.

When we got in that afternoon there was a hand from headquarters with Carlton's mail and some groceries. As I helped unload the pickup, Carlton grained the horses and finished his outside chores. The cowboy from headquarters told me how lucky I was to get on this particular camp. All the single guys wanted to work here just for the food. It seemed like I was living with the best cook west of the Mississippi. I thought to myself, "If the food here is considered that great, them poor boys down at headquarters must be goin' through pure hell." Then he told me the rest of the story.

It seems that Carlton grew up in this area, and was a pretty good cowboy, but he always wanted to be a chef. No one really took him seriously about his wanting to cook, because he was always pulling little jokes and messing with someone's mind. So when he quit his job and went to cooking school, everyone just figured he was hunting new range. But after hard work and lots of classes Carlton finally managed to get a job in New Orleans in a big fine restaurant. In about six years he got the job as head hash-slinger. After about twelve years as the head chef, he just got tired of his job and came back home. He hadn't changed much, just put on a little weight, but he had gotten ten times worse at messing with people's minds.

I had been had. The hand went back to headquarters, and I went to thinking. By supper time I had me a plan, and after a meal of fried stuff that couldn't be recognized even after the black had been scraped away, I set my plan into action.

123

I washed the dishes pretty much the same way as always, except for the fact that I used a little extra soap, and when I rinsed the dishes I used cold water on half the plates. And when I put them up I stacked them in a special order. I suffered through breakfast, dinner, and supper again. Each time the meal was worse, and each time there was just a tad more soap left on half the dishes.

After breakfast on the second day, we rode out to do our rat killin'. We split up to see what we could find, and planned to meet at the branding pens. From there we could gather on our way back to camp. I made it to the pens about 1:30, and noticed that Carlton was already there. As I rode up I saw him take his pants off the top rail of the corral, and start putting them on. I could see that he was kinda upset. His eyes were sunk back in his head, and he was walking like he might be a little saddle sore. When I stepped off to get myself a drink and to roll me a smoke, Carlton eased over to me and said, "Pard, we need to have us a talk."

I got a drink of water, rolled a smoke, and leaned back against the windmill tower. Grinning, I said, "So talk." Carlton worked his way around so he was standing in the sun, so his Levis could dry some more, took a deep breath, and started.

"Ya know, kid, I don't want you to take this the wrong way or anything like that, 'cause I think you're doin' one helluva job of dish-washin'. But I got to thinkin', just this mornin', that I may have been sluffin' off on my cookin' duties just a mite. Now I might just be able to come up with a few decent meals once in a while, if you could see your way clear to get just a touch more soap off of those dishes. I haven't had the scours this bad since me and my cousin drank all that home brew and ate that half bushel of wild plums. Hell, I haven't been able to ride more'n half a mile without havin' to stop and tend to business. As you can see, I was a little slow gettin' off my horse the last time and I had to wash my Levis out at the windmill. Now since we've had this little talk, let's get on back to camp."

From that time on I ate some of the best groceries ever, and Carlton even started talking. When I quit and went looking for newer range I had a tactic to use on the next cook that wouldn't.[27]

Without Cosi, the chuck wagon cook, the roundup, the trail drive, and the whole cattle industry could not have been what it was. The cowboys often cussed the chuck and the cook, called him names like Vinegar Jim and Bilious Bill and Dirty Dave—not to mention some less polite handles.[28] But on a dry drive, when the cowboys were working the clock around to keep the steers moving north, the cook kept open house all night long, with food and Arbuckles' to keep the waddies going. He knew that hardship is easier to bear if the hands are well fed.[29] And on more normal nights, when the cook had put a lighted lantern on the tip of the wagon tongue to guide the night crews back to the outfit, and pointed the wagon toward the North Star to provide bearings for the next day's drive,[30] it was easy to remember that the chuck wagon was home, and the chuck wagon cook—irascible though he might be—was in some ways the heart and soul of the outfit.

MAHOMET AND TH' MOUNT.

CHAPTER SIX

There's Something Going On Every Day

The everydayness of the cowboy's life, which pro-duced the boredom already discussed, was also the source of a great deal of humor, sometimes unintended, and sometimes the natural consequence of the ups and downs of the waddies' lives. They did all they could on horseback, and resented vigorously having to grease windmills or "juice" cows. (In fact, one of the descriptions of Texas that I grew up with was an enumeration following a pattern: Texas has more X and less Y than anyplace else, etc., etc.—and one naturally occurring item was "more cows and less milk.")

Elmer Kelton, in a memorable scene, has one of his "good old boys," accompanied by his teenage nephews, driving a small herd of horses toward a corral gate, hoping

to pen them up for the night. A fellow lounging near the gate—less than a hundred yards from it—got up, saddled his horse, and rode over to open the gate. It took more time for him to saddle his horse than it would have taken to walk the short distance—but a cowboy never walks when he can ride. The incoming folks then knew for sure that the gate-opener was really a cowboy.[1] Such a habit is not to be confused with the folks out in Arizona who reportedly go fishing cowboy-style—on horseback. The only risk is that if you cast a hook and snag your horse's rump, look out! Of course two cowboy fishers can team-cast, one hooking the fish by the head, the other by the tail; then they hogtie it, two fins and a tail.[2] Do you believe that?

The cowboy did get off his horse at times, like when he went to town. Especially at the end of a trail drive, when the boys had not seen a woman nor a bottle of whiskey for months, the cowboy navigated the streets of Dodge or Abilene or Ogallala on his own. But even here there are exceptions: like the drummer in Sam Murray's saloon in Sheffield, Texas, who was

> enjoying a quiet drink when a cowboy, wheeling
> his horse away from the bar, caused the critter
> to stomp on the drummer's foot. Immediately
> the drummer took his complaint to the bar-
> tender, who was Sam Murray himself. But there
> was no sympathy, much less compensation,
> forthcoming from Sam.
> "What the hell you a-doin' in here afoot any-
> how?" he asked.[3]

Such an event is what "Teddy Blue" (E.C. Abbott) would have grouped with "lots of big doings that did not amount

to much in a serious way, but made good stories to tell up
and down the range."[4] And the tales that came out of trips
to town are certainly rich for whiling away boring hours.
One such is of truly folk character—the cowboy at the
melodrama who mistook acting for reality:

> We all got well lit up and went to a hot show on
> Blake Street. The play I think was called "Poor
> Nell"; anyway, a burglar beats his wife to death
> on the stage. After he knocked her down he
> taken hold of her hair and beat her head on the
> floor, and every time he struck her head he
> would stamp his foot. It sounded like her head
> hitting the floor, but it wasn't her head at all. I
> was sober enough to know that. But some of
> them weren't. Bill Roden, one of the cowboys,
> had went to sleep but the noise woke him up,
> and the first thing he saw was the man beating
> the woman's head on the floor. We sat right in
> front, and he gave one jump onto the stage and
> busted the fellow on the head with his six-gun
> before he remembered where he was. The
> woman got up and began to cuss him, all hell
> broke loose, somebody pulled Bill off the stage,
> they called for the police, the boys shot out the
> lights, and everybody broke their necks getting
> away from there.[5]

A very similar story involves a play being performed in
Waxahatchie, Texas, by a traveling company. As I recall the
tale, the company's leading lady had been taken sick, and
one of the local ladies of the evening was put in her place.
When the dastardly villain, in a fit of drunken rage, shot

her and she fell dead on the stage, the remorseful villain cried out, "What have I done?" A cowboy in the audience said, loud enough for all the audience to hear, "You've just killed the best whore in Waxahatchie!"[6]

Huck Finn's visit to the circus, when he mistook a "drunk" trying to ride a prancing horse for a real human being in trouble, involved just such a confusion of illusion with reality.[7] But cowboys at a St. Paul circus were right at home when anyone in the crowd was challenged by a clown to ride his trick mule. The boys picked out their best rider, determined to win the promised five dollars, and supplied him with Texas spurs—which he proceeded to rake the mule with, while hitting it with his hat.

> There were thousands of people in the audience
> to witness the stunt. The mule made two or
> three jumps and roared like a mountain lion and
> our rider yelled like a Comanche Indian; the
> mule would pitch and roar, but our rider stuck
> to him like a postage stamp. As the rider could
> not be dismounted the mule laid down on the
> ground and rolled over like a ball. Our rider
> stood by, and when the mule would get on his
> feet he would find our rider on his back until,
> finally, the mule sulled and just stood in the mid-
> dle of the ring with our rider still on him spur-
> ring and whipping him with his hat.

That mule had apparently never met a Texas cowboy before. The crowd went wild, and the police had to be called to get the rider off the mule—but the five dollars was paid, and likely it got spent at the nearest saloon.[8] That story doubtless got good mileage, as well as a bit of enlargement, when the boys got home.

Joseph G. McCoy, the pioneer cattle shipper who wrote a classic of the cattle trailing industry in 1874, described graphically the cowboy hilarity at the end of the trail, telling it like it was during the height of the trail drive era:

> When the herd is sold and delivered to the purchaser, a day of rejoicing to the cow-boy has come, for then he can go free and have a jolly time. [After getting bathed, shaved, and dressed in new clothes from top to toe, he is ready] for fun and frolic. The bar-room, the theatre, the gambling room, the bawdy house, the dance house, each and all come in for their full share of attention. [The women at trail's end are terribly wicked.] When the darkness of night is come to shroud their orgies from public gaze, these miserable beings gather into the halls of the dance house, and "trip the fantastic toe" to wretched music, ground out of dilapidated instruments, by beings fully as degraded as the most vile. In this vortex of dissipation the average cow-boy plunges with great delight.[9]

One would gather that Mr. McCoy did not so plunge in—but the cowboys did, with vigor.

Teddy Blue was thus employed in having a jolly time when he got his name, and the story followed him all his life. He was drinking with a young lady dressed in circus tights "that looked like she had been melted and run into them." He turned down her offer to buy a bottle of overpriced wine, but then she invited him to go up to her room.

That sounded better to me and I was going to
go. But there was a dark hall that ran around
behind the stage, and as we started along it I
remembered that I had seven hundred dollars
on me, in my six-shooter belt. Part of it was left
over from that money I inherited, and besides I
was drawing top hand's wages, seventy-five dollars a month, and I had all that money too. And
I thought there might be some kind of a deadfall
back there—I was a wise guy—I'd heard those
stories.

So I turned around, and as I turned my spur
catched on a carpet and I fell through a thin
partition onto the stage. Well, I thought, if
you're before an audience you've got to do
something, so I grabbed a chair from one of the
musicians and straddled it and bucked it all
around the stage, yelling, "Whoa, Blue! Whoa,
Blue!"—which was a cowpuncher expression at
that time. Before they even got me off the stage
it had started. The manager yelled, "Hey, Blue,
come out of there," and the audience was yelling
with laughter and they took it up. And when I
went out of that theatre that night I was Blue,
and Teddy Blue I have been for fifty-five years.[10]

Teddy might be said to have been on the stage, but his
skills as a performer were somewhat lacking. Another
escapade that enlivened many a dull time with its retelling
was an evening he spent in a parlor house in Miles City,
Montana:

Three of us was in the parlor of Maggie Burns's

house giving a song number called "The Texas Ranger." John Bowen was playing the piano and he couldn't play the piano, and Johnny Stringfellow was there sawing on a fiddle and he couldn't play a fiddle, and I was singing, and between the three of us we was raising the roof. And Maggie—the fighting, red-headed son of a gun—got hopping mad and says: "If you leather-legged sons of bitches want to give a concert, why don't you hire a hall? You're ruining my piano."

So I got mad, too, and I says: "If I had little Billy here"—well, I told her what I'd do to her piano. And John Bowen said: "Go and get him, Teddy, go and get him." That was enough for me. I went across the street and got Billy out of the livery stable, and came back and rode him through the hall and into the parlor, where I dismounted. And as soon as I got in the parlor, Maggie slammed the door and locked it, and called the police.

But there was a big window in the room, that was low to the ground, and Billy and me got through it and got away. We headed for the ferry on a dead run, and that is the origin of the story that Charlie Russell tells in *Rawhide Rawlins,* about me telling that jackrabbit to "get out of the way, brother, and let a fellow run that can run." I got to the ferry just as it was pulling out, and jumped little Billy across a little piece of water onto the apron. The sheriff got there right after me and he was hollering at the ferryman to stop. And the ferryman hollered back at him: "This feller has got a gun the size of a stovepipe stuck in my ribs, and I ain't a-going to stop."[11]

One might assume that Teddy and his friends had been drinking. Another cowboy had partaken of the cup that cheers in town, and apparently had more than he could handle:

> Late in the afternoon the sheriff saw the cowboy walking down the street, apparently unaware that he was walking with one foot up on the curb and the other in the gutter. The sheriff pulled up alongside him and said, "Hey, cowboy. Did you realize that you're walking with one foot on the curb and the other in the gutter?" The cowboy gave the sheriff a weak, somewhat drunken smile and said, "Thank God! I thought I had been crippled."[12]

Along the same line is the story of the cowboy who had been on a spree, drinking in a saloon and singing "The Old Chisholm Trail" till the bartender ran him off.

> But this cowboy was enjoyin' life, and nothin' seemed to make 'im mad. The saloon was built high, with a wooden porch 'bout five feet from the ground and with wide steps that led to the street and hitch rack below. As he came through the swingin' doors to make his way across the street to 'nother bar where his welcome hadn't been wore out, he was liftin' his feet like a sandhill crane walkin' up a riverbed. Halfway across the porch he let go with his acid tenor to continue the song he'd started inside:

"With my knees in the saddle an' my seat
in the sky-y-y,
I'll quit punchin' cattle in the sweet by an'
by-y-y-y."

Jes' then he missed the steps and landed five feet below, the jar rattlin' his bones like throwin' down an armload of wood, but he kept standin' straight up. With hardly a break in his song, he continued in correct time and rhythm:

"An', by God, they shore built them steps
damned high-h-h-h."[13]

Another cowboy on a binge figured out a way to comply with the law against carrying a pistol into Pecos, Texas. He tied it to a rope and dragged it behind him all over the town, hollering out, "Don't step on my tail, boys. Open the door an' let me an' my tail through!"[14]

One herd owner was apparently kin to the puritanical cattle shipper Joseph McCoy: he wouldn't let his men have a copy of the *Police Gazette* (that early-day equivalent of today's racy men's magazines, complete with illustrations of dancing girls in tights), forbade his trail crew to drink when they hit Miles City, and went in to keep his eye on them, sitting in the hotel lobby where he had a good view. One of the boys, who knew the famous (infamous?) Calamity Jane—the wildest of Western women—offered her two and a half to go sit in the old man's lap and kiss him, right there before God and everybody. Well, she did it up brown, throwed both her arms around him so his arms were pinned to his sides and he couldn't help himself—she was strong as a bear. And then she began kissing him and saying "Why don't you ever come see me any more, honey? You know I love you." And so forth. The fellow that put Calamity up to it went and told the old man,

"Go ahead. Have a good time. It's customary here. I won't write home and tell your folks about it."

The old man spluttered and spit and wiped his mouth on his handkerchief. And he left the hotel and that was the last we saw of him that night.[15]

While that story was based upon a common need—to get rid of the "house mother" so the good times could roll—just plain fun was involved in another put-up job. The Frontier Days in Prescott, Arizona, were in full swing, and one of the boys was parading "down Whiskey Row with his best girl riding by his side. On signal, all the upper-story windows of Prescott's sporting houses flew open, and the soiled doves yelled at the cowboy, 'Hello, honey'!"[16] Nobody needed to write home reporting that one.

A story that is similarly juvenile—but clean—involves a couple of teenage cowboys who wanted to attend a rodeo a couple of hundred miles from home, but Daddy told 'em to stay home and tend to their business:

They'd been chousing around the country to rodeos all summer, and it was his firm belief they'd better stay at the ranch and do a little practical work for a change. In fact, he added, that was an order and it had damn sure better be followed.

But like all boys, they occasionally went against parental decree. And they chose this ill-fated time to disobey the old man. Off they drove, when he was out of sight, in a fine new station wagon. They arrived safely at the rodeo, did it full justice, and returned to their station wagon to find they'd locked the keys inside. All they could think of to do at the moment was knock out a window and retrieve the keys.

Being none too well supplied with money, or considering money wasted when spent for room rent, they decided to sleep in the station wagon. They carefully hung their clothes on the steering wheel and other suitable gadgets and went to sleep. In the morning—Ay, Chihuahua!—their clothes were gone. Some fiendish thief had walked off with them.

Then, as if this disaster weren't sufficiently disastrous, here came their daddy. It seems he, too, had decided to attend the rodeo.

The family reunion failed to establish a new record for filial joy, but actually it wasn't too bad. Although the boys had been disobedient, they were definitely in a jam, what with Society's narrow-minded attitude toward proper apparel, not to mention the discomfort of being half-naked in a station wagon with a busted window. The father helped the boys round up some clothes, taking them in his own car to do so. Then the boys started home, agreeing to stop at a certain restaurant en route and have lunch with their father, who would be following them.

At the lunch stop they waited and waited and

wondered why the old man was so late. Finally
one of the boys, in the process of getting some
money out of his pocket for the jukebox, discovered why his dad hadn't shown. He had his
dad's keys in his pocket.[17]

Once a man showed up in Frank Ward's saloon in Denver
with a rattlesnake in a big glass jar, offering to sell it to the
owner. He pointed out that it would attract a lot of attention, and bet that nobody could keep his finger on the jar
when the snake struck. One of the boys bet drinks for the
house that he could do it, knowing that the snake couldn't
possibly strike him through the glass. But reflexes took
over, and he lost, time and again, to the tune of seventeen
dollars. So Frank bought the snake, and made money on
it—till some hothead, sore at losing his bet, broke the jar
and the snake got out and had to be killed.[18]

A couple of quickies about wayward husbands in town
are worth sharing. One involves a fellow from Sonora,
Texas, whose wife suspected he wasn't simply attending
the Fort Worth Stock Show, so she hired a detective to
follow him. When he got home a week later, she cornered
him: "I've got the goods on you this time. I've had a private
detective trailing every step while you were gone!"

"Well, I'll tell you something," he replied. "That detective
is one tired son-of-a-buck!"

And a San Angelo rancher went to the Fort Worth Stock
Show, planning to buy some Angus bulls.

He and another ranching buddy also tried to
forget the woes of ranching while they were
there. [After a little toot—or maybe it was a big
one—he called his wife to explain his delayed

139

return:] "Honey, I've got some bulls bought, but I'm having trouble getting a truck. I may be a day or two late getting home."

"Now that's strange," she said with hardly any warmth, "the truck got here with your bulls about two hours ago."[19]

And now one final cowboy-in-town tale: Sam Lawrence and Teddy Blue and some of the boys delivered a herd to Chicago, and in their explorations of the Windy City ran into "Madame Somebody's Waxworks. For Men Only." So they went in. Teddy tells what happened:

There was a man standing at the door and he handed me a box of snuff—I said: "No, thank you," and walked on, before I noticed that he was part of the show. Pretty soon we came to a sort of show window, and inside was a woman leaning away over, with one foot stuck straight up in the air and a globe spinning around on it, and the other foot stuck out behind her. All she had on was a little black velvet G-string.

I was standing right next to her and I could hear her tick. But Sam was further away, and his vision was blurred anyhow, and he thought it was real. He said: "Poor little girl! The idea of a man making a woman do a thing like that before all these men! Why, hanging's too good for him." And he went on like that, working himself up.

I said, "Hold on, Sam. This is a waxworks lay-out. She's wound up." And I laid my hand on the leg that was stuck out behind her, to convince him.

He said: "The trouble with you you've lived with these no'thern-raised sons of bitches so long you don't respect a woman yourself."

Well, you take them out of the saddle and that's what they are.[20]

I imagine that experience made the rounds back home, but memorable events were taking place there too, to be treasured and shared. For example, the old trick of creasing a horse—shooting it glancingly on a certain place on the neck or head, to knock it temporarily unconscious—finds its way into a number of events, and the results are not always those desired. Nora Ramírez collected such a story from an old New Mexico rancher:

There was a group of wild horses . . . and Kurt wanted a little bay mare. Ever' day he'd say, "I shore do want to get that mare!" So we decided we'd crease her. So we got her run up under one of them high bluffs in a little cove. She was lookin' right straight at us so I was gonna crease her. But Ole Kurt he says, "Aw, you never could shoot. Let me crease her." So he grabs that gun and he wasn't over fifty yards from her. We was peekin' over the rocks so Ole Kurt he even rested his gun on a rock. She just dropped like that when he shot. We bullfrogged off that bluff, to hurry down there and tie her. Went down there and turned her head around and Ole Kurt had shot her square between the eyes. Didn't crease her a'tall.[21]

141

Philip Rollins said that the practice of creasing was overreported, and that "as usually attempted, [it] resulted in entirely missing the animal, or in killing him." It was only rarely attempted "legitimately," he says, by desperate men who were afoot in waterless country.[22]

A shooting that was not meant to involve creasing once caused a small Indian uprising. A Cheyenne named Black Wolf came visiting a couple of Montana ranchers and was given dinner, after which he went out and sat in the sun, napping, with his tall stovepipe hat on. One of the ranchers bet he could shoot a hole through the Indian's hat without touching his head—but he missed. The bullet creased Black Wolf, knocking him unconscious. The ranchers thought he was dead and rode on to the next ranch for help, sure that it would be needed when the rest of the Cheyennes found out what they had done. Black Wolf came to, went for his tribal members, and they came back. After running the ranchers and friends off, shooting the dog, and burning the ranch house, they called it even—but the man who did the creasing left the country for good. The Indians were arrested, but treated fairly, and after an investigation, they were released. But it could have been quite serious.[23]

Serious enough for the participants was an experience that Paul Patterson had back in the '30s when the night horse got away—that was the horse kept staked out so the crew would have a mount to round up the rest of the saddle horses in the morning. The story is famous in the Pecos River country of Texas, and Paul tried his hand at turning it into verse:

Night Horse Nightmare
BY PAUL PATTERSON

> Time: Breakin' daylight, Easter nineteen-thirty-
> one;

Place: West-of-the-Pecos horse ranch—bachelor-
    run;
Cast of Characters: Approximately three:
Straw Boss Cutter, ol' Bill Wyatt, and me.

Breakfast table: Setting and Scene;
A sadder sight is seldom seen;
Grim and glum and right tight-lipped,
There we set with coffee *un*sipped.

Elbows on table and faces dropped;
Flapjacks cold and syrup *un*sopped;
There we set with spirits *trampled,*
Gravy cold and sowbelly *un*sampled.

So, what on earth could the matter be
In the bachelor home of this once-happy three?
What's all this saddened silence about?
Now I ain't one bad news to shout
That the night horse Buster has done went and
    got out!

I cannot straight from the shoulder shoot:
My chicken style is to *circumlocute: say like*
Twelve hunderd horses this outfit runs
But haf to depend on jist this one;
But as of rat now cain't depend on *none!*

That dad dam Buster—now don't blame me—
Has slid the gate latch and set his self free!

Cutter flinched as if popped with a hot shot;
Bill tipped over the coffee pot!

A cowboy reduced to his own two feet?
Worse'n a croton-oiled cat on solid concrete;
A cowboy afoot and out of breath;
Worse'n a frontier female's fate worse than
    death.

Now Bill jumped up all a-flame and a-fluster;
Says, "Ah'm takin muh thirty thirty to that
    damn Buster."
"Bill, crease him too low, you're afoot and in a
    jam."
"But no more afooter'n I I-God am."

I set there sayin' neither yay nor nay
In eager anticipation of a *horseless* day;
Thirteen hours and a sixty-mile ride;
Hell on tender tendons and hiney hide!

Then Bill says

"Won't get nowheres on idle talk
And Ah'll be damned if Ah'm gonna walk;
So, Cutter, rat now Ah'm here to say
We're buildin' to Buster in mah Green Dodge
    Cuepay:
She's sound of bottom and right fraish shod
And can go anywhere a hoss has trod!"

Cutter, still part of the horse frontier,
Gazed on car critter with tremblin' and fear;
'Specially when he learnt he was to saddle the
    car's hood
And whip a loop on Buster as soon as he could.

Now a word about Buster, AWOL night hoss
Over us three bachelors now total boss;
Long, anvil head, one shoebutton eye;
For registry papers he need not apply.

Flitter-flat feet and feathered fetlocks
Bespoke of breeding a mite unorthodox;
A geldin', of course, but cut somewhat proud,
With much more drive than nature allowed—

Sex drive, that is—and as a consequence
We spotted Buster prancin' the horse-trap fence,
Psychin' hisself up with long, lustful stares
At Kempland's manada of shapely young mares!

Here the hoss race opened and opened good;
One hoss on hoof versus forty under hood.
From the very jump go the one hoss won;
For a pudd'n-footed part Perch'un that booger
    could run.

Head high, to the side, tail figger nine
He left Green Dodger a good ways behind,
Some thirty yards back and still losin' ground

145

But bearin' the brunt of Buster's insultin' sounds.

This don't mean to say *we* weren't in the run-
　　nin';
Footfeed on floor, ol' Bill was gunnin';
Me? head under arms and eyelids glued tight
To blot out that rump-bumpin', stump-jumpin',
　　frightenin' sight.

"To hell with Buster, slow this thing down,
Turn rat around and take me to town!"
"Settle down, Paul, we won't hub no stump!"
"Don't make a damn now, I'm fixin' to jump!"

Cutter so busy ridin' the coupe
Lost all interest in castin' his loop.
The far far behind Cuepay still showed class,
Still matchin' Buster in emission of gas.

We waltzed that Buster around and around
When all of a suddent, Dodger run aground,
(With ever' indication of a hip knocked down.)

Now she just set there and steamed and boiled
Emittin' sundry waters, gases and oils;
Yep, pore Dodger had run her course;
That dad dam Buster was too much horse,

Head still cocked and feet still a-thunder,

Tail figger nine, and emissions from thereunder.
We tried one round afoot—how bitter the dose.
Agin that Buster it wasn't even close.

Warn't superior smarts brought Buster to book:
It was them dirty-mean tackticks we took.
We wired shut the gate leading to the trough
And shut pore Buster's water off!

Buster, Bill, and Cutter—across that Great Divide;
But here I am, still on Buster's side.
'Cause someday, somewhere, comes my end;
I'm gonna need Buster as man's best friend.

A final word—to St. Peter:
Check that Pearly Gate agin—and agin—
Or that dam Buster'll be gettin' out—
Or, most likely, gettin' in.[24]

That "no more afooter'n I I-God am" seems to capture a genuine feeling of desperation. I think they should have let Bill try creasing ole Buster, under the circumstances. Or, given a bit more modern scene, a different ending might have been in order:

You seldom see a cowboy a-horseback or a
horse afoot nowadays—both commute to work
in a car and trailer. Indicative of this trend is the
story of the cowboy and his pet horse who are

making the transition together. And it is coming much easier for the horse.

Anyhow, the two have ridden to the back side of the pasture, gotten out, and started their cow work in the old cowboy manner. The old pony, suddenly feeling his oats, downs his head and throws the old cowboy off, as was the case when both were younger. And, as was the case, the old cowboy would be forced to walk home.

But this time, the horse upon throwing the cowboy off, runs and jumps back into the trailer, ready to go to the house. The cowboy picks himself up, painfully hobbles over to the trailer, kicks the old pony out, gets in his car and drives off. Once under way he hollers back at the critter:

"Now, damn ye, you walk home!"[25]

Other problems of the working cowboy also produce situations retold with humor—like the cowboy who had lost so much sleep that he swore he was going to move to Greenland, where the nights are six months long—and even there, he said, he wouldn't get up till noon![26] And the rancher who swears that every maverick (unbranded calf not following its mother) is the offspring of "Old Crump," and the cowboys have to be prepared to back the boss up. Old Crump had more calves in one year than any other over-age cow in history![27] And when a cowboy is late relieving the person riding herd on the cattle—habitually late—there's a cure:

Uncle Fisher Pollard once took drastic measures against a cowboy who consistently and persistently relieved him late. One cold night he pitched a loop to his guard partner, who secured the same to the tarp-covered cowboy still sleeping in his wind-protected spot. Wheeling off at right angles, Uncle Fish spurred for a fast fifty yards across the lumpy, bumpy plains. Thereafter he was promptly, if not sooner, relieved at guard.[28]

Even with all the discomforts of range life, the cowboy generally took things in stride, and was completely loyal to the outfit as long as he was working for it. He might go two days without sleep, grab a few hours rest on wet saddle blankets in the rain, and get up happy. The only things that a cowboy couldn't handle was being set afoot—and being around a decent woman.[29] Of course, there was always the exception, like the temptation a young cowboy faced on the trail to Kansas who was sent to buy some milk at a nearby nester's[30] cabin.

They gave me a dollar and sent me to bargain with the nester's wife for a bucketful. When I got to the house, there was no one there but the lady herself. She filled my bucket, and just as she handed it up where I sat on my horse, I winked at her. I knew she didn't like it. In fact, after I went back to camp, she sent her husband with a shotgun to tell me so.

"Where's the kid that came after the milk?" he growled. I thought my goose was cooked, but some of the boys told him I was off with the herd. But when he saw me, he insisted that I was the bird that had winked at his wife, and he intended to make use of me in a little target practice. If someone hadn't told him that winkin' was a nervous defect of my eyes—just a nervous twitching that I couldn't help, I suppose I would have been buzzard bait. He didn't seem very convinced about it and stuck around to see. I nearly wore my left eye out trying to prove it. He followed us a piece when we broke herd, and I winked and winked. Finally he turned his horse back home.

"Well, I guess the son-of-a-gun couldn't help it," he said and left us. But after we returned that way from Kansas, we met him again, and I had to wink some more. I guess he'd have killed me if I hadn't kept it going.[31]

A small wager might be placed confidently that the winker got a nickname—Winkie, for instance—that he was years living down.

In another case where quick thinking got a man out of trouble, a fellow got word that another had called him a son of a bitch. The accused had an answer that seemed to satisfy everyone: "I never said you were a son of a bitch. I don't know how folks found out."[32]

And in that worst of all jobs, windmilling, situations develop that produce humorous tales worth repeating—like the time two cowboys were working on a mill and one dropped a monkey wrench, which bounced off the head of the man below. The man in the tower hollered—too late—"Look out!" The man below said, "What the hell you gonna do? Th'ow another one?" And in another case, the man working in the tower lost his grip and fell on the other cowboy, knocking both of them to the ground. The man on the bottom said, with some vigor, "You crazy son-of-a-bitch, don't you know you can kill a man—fallin' off a windmill on him?"[33]

Somewhat related to windmills is the tale of Mack, the Patterson vehicle of mixed parentage. After a lot of encouragement from Paul, Ralph, and John, Mr. Patterson had finally traded for a truck chassis and engine which was "added to"—

Although the label on the radiator said "Ford," it was of the mongrel breed. . . . Buick rear, Chevrolet universal, etc., with strains of Hupmobile, Apperson Jackrabbit, and Cole Eight blood in evidence here and there. In deference to Henry Ford, and because we'd gotten the majority from Dr. McDonald, we called it Mack.

So here we are rattling down the road. Ralph had relinquished the steering wheel to Papa because of the latter's desperate need to become attuned to the machine age. What with Ralph in close attendance, and deep ruts to simplify steering, Papa ought to make it all right. Even so, Ralph had his misgivings. And rightly so, for when a big wooden gate loomed up it took all of Papa's strength and Ralph's ingenuity to get Old Mack to "whoa."

John jumped out, or rather off, to open the gate. Just as he got it pointed directly at us, Old Mack cold-jawed, or something, on Papa, and lunged into the one-by-four that served as a latch, gave a coughing, gurgling sound, and died. But the gurgling sound continued. The gate latch had stabbed open Mack's bladder.

"What's it look like?" Papa asked, his tone three quarters in anger, one quarter in shame,

since he felt some blame for Old Mack's lurch-
ing. John's reply was one to bring joy to any
Westerner that ever lived, if the inquiry per-
tained to a brand new well and windmill on his
property. But on this occasion it fell on unappreciative ears.

"Oh, Papa, it's throwin' a fine stream."[34]

Then there's the old story about the man with a name for
being ugly. He said publicly—and often—that if he ever
found a man who was uglier than he was, he would shoot
him. As the standard story goes, when he finally met such a
fellow, the second man said, "By God, if I'm uglier than
you, shoot!" Another version goes, "If I'm uglier than you,
you won't have to shoot me; I'll do it myself!"[35]

A story that fails to fit any particular category, but is
retold frequently with variations, has to do with the cowboys who were swapping yarns about the most pain they
had ever endured. One topped everyone else with his story
of having been out on the plains when he had to relieve
himself. He had the misfortune to lower his bared rear end
over a big bear trap, which snapped shut on him. "Lordy,"
one of the other boys said, "I'll bet that really hurt." "Not as
much as it did when I hit the end of the chain," he said.[36]

Among the pastimes of the cowboy, as discussed earlier,
was the all-time favorite—the ranch dance. Folks would
ride, or drive in buggies and wagons, for miles to take part,
and since women were generally in short supply, men had
to dance "lady fashion" to make up the lack. They were
"heifer branded" with a handkerchief tied around the upper arm.[37] One old-timer's reminiscences recounted such an
event that went beyond the usual. Jake de Puyster, a six-
foot-two blond giant, had a buddy, Buck, who wasn't having any luck at all managing for a dance with one of the

few ladies present. Jake told him to hang on, not to go home, and he assured Buck that a "she-pardner" to dance with him would appear.

Ten minutes later he returned, bringing Buck a partner that stopped drinking, dance, and play—the most remarkably clad figure that ever entered even a frontier dance-hall.

Still wearing his usual costume—wide chaps, spurred heels, and belt—having removed nothing but his tall-crowned Mexican sombrero, Jake had mavericked three certain articles of feminine apparel and contrived to get himself into same.

Cocked jauntily over his right eye he wore a bright red toque crowned with a faded wreath of pale blue flowers, from which a bedraggled green feather drooped wearily over his left ear; about his waist wrinkled a broad pink sash, tied in a great double bow-knot set squarely in front, while fastened also about his waist, pendent no more than midway of his long thighs, hung a garment white of colour, filmy of fabric, bifurcated of form, richly ruffled to extremity—so habited came Jake, and, with a broad grin lurking within the mazes of his great bushy beard and monstrous moustache, sidled mincingly to his mate and shyly murmured a hint he might have the privilege of the next quadrille.

At first Buck was furious, growled, and swore to kill Jake for the insult, until, infected by the gales of laughter that swept the room, he awkwardly offered his arm and led his weird partner to an unfilled set.

A sorry hour was this to the other ladies; for,
while there were better dancers and prettier,
that first quadrille made "Miss De Puyster" the
belle of the ball for the rest of the day and night,
and not a few serious affrays over disputes for
an early chance of a "round" or "square" with
her were narrowly avoided.

After a while Buck introduced his partner with an interesting assessment of her charms:

"Fellers, this here is Miss De Puyster; she ain't
much for pritty, but she's hell for active on the
floor—so dodburned active I couldn't tell
whether she was waltzin' or tryin' to throw me
side-holts."[38]

Teddy Blue said this event really took place with a fellow
with a very similar name—Jake De Rosses—doing the
dressing up, at a honky-tonk dance in Ogallala, mentioning
that it "even got into books"—citing the above account.
And, according to Teddy's autobiography, he was himself
urged by Cowboy Annie, one of the Lincoln, Nebraska,
girls, to pull on a pair of women's drawers—Annie's, which
she took off for the occasion—over his britches and to
parade down the street with her. He even kept the drawers
as a trophy, later carrying them like a flag as he traveled to
a new camp, and then hanging them on the wall of his
cabin. Later one of the boys tore them down and put them
in the stove, because they "wasn't decent." Teddy agreed,
but he was a long time sober by then.[39]
Cowboys high jinks at dances were not limited to provid-

ing "heifers" for substitute partners. One report says that the "new beginner" who wanted to learn to dance was the subject of much hilarity:

> All care was given to get him "balled up." Some of the girls were unusually strong, and when they swung the "new beginner," they would sometimes send him reeling against the wall; the dance was prolonged beyond its usual length for his special benefit, that he might get "blowed" or "winded."[40]

This story reminds me of my own earlier days. A group that I used to square-dance with in Lubbock, Texas, in the 1950s, had a lot of fun telling others about my exuberance in swinging a certain lady. She was petite, and a real beauty, but I noticed that when I danced with her, there seemed to be an extra amount of laughter in our corner of the hall. Puzzled, I asked around till I found out that, without realizing it, every time I'd swing her I lifted her feet off the floor for several inches, and she went flying through the air. She never complained, and I never quit dancing with her, nor swinging her the usual way. But whenever I went over to ask her to dance, there would always be a half-dozen giggles from the smart-alecks around who had heard the story.

From the ranch dance to cowboy singing is only a little step—and there continues to be the question about whether or not the cowboys sang the herd to sleep at night. Most authorities agree that few cowboys had lovely voices, but the consensus seems to be that they had to make some kind of noise at night to let the cattle know all was well. A low hum or whistle often served the purpose, so that the sleeping herd wouldn't be startled by the sudden noise of a horse shaking itself, which, considering all the pieces of leather overlapping on a saddle, could make quite a noise. But there was an additional reason for singing or whistling—safety. One man went down during a stampede and when daylight came, it was found that the cowboys had unknowingly run the herd over his body repeatedly during the night. After that, it was customary to sing or whistle while trying to stop a stampede; if the sound stopped, someone went to see what had happened.[41]

After this grim beginning, a little humor would likely be in order. Such comes in the form of the story of Fall-Back Joe's singing. A horse wrangler and fine roper, Joe was badly crippled, his left leg being some six inches shorter than the other. He had to mount his horse "Injun fashion," on the right side, and he had to train his horses to accept this unaccustomed way of doing things.

Fall-Back Joe, being a horse wrangler, had no night guarding to do, which was strictly according to cowboy etiquette. That didn't keep him from singing, however. One of his "favor-ites" was "Lorena," that popular old-time ballad, sentimental and sad to the very last degree. Some puncher once said that he "would be willing to bet a pair of Coffeyville boots agin a left-handed sock that Lorena had sung more cows to sleep an' stopped more about-to-happen stampedes than all the other songs put together."

Frequently in the evening Fall-Back Joe would sit round the camp fire and sing for some time, and Lorena always opened the program. Naturally the words and music of this famous song were picked up by every man with the wagon, and it was sung so many times and under so many circumstances day and night that Rickety Bob, the cranky cook, finally announced in no uncertain tones that, excepting Fall-Back Joe, he, Rickety Bob, proposed to take the pothook and beat up the very first puncher who even hummed the tune around the wagon.

Joe's voice escaped from the opening beneath his mustache at one corner and was of a most distressingly nasal character. The Chinese cook at the ranch of an English company had an exact duplicate of the limping horse wrangler's vocal organs. It certainly was something awful in the line of a singing voice. I can see and hear Joe right now, sitting on a bed roll by the fire, making a pure wreck of Lorena musically and poetically:

Lorena

Oh, the years creep slowly by, Lorena.
The snow is on the grass again.
The sun's low down in the sky, Lorena.
The frost gleams where the stars have
    been.

Joe always called her "Lorener" and pronounced "been" to rhyme with "bean."

"Lorena" was essentially a song of a sad and weepy heart, and Joe and his imitators always pulled out the tremolo stop right at the start and kept it out to the very last quavering word:

A hundred months have passed, Lorena,
Since last I held that hand in mine,
And felt that pulse beat fast, Lorena,
Though mine beat faster far than thine.

Rickety Bob allowed, he did, that "a hundred months, meanin' nigh onto eight and a third years, was a powerful long time to re-co-lect a gal's pulse." Bob also reckoned it was a long, long time to stick to the woman. He was sure that Lorena was probably married and had at least three kids by this time. Such sarcasm was wholly lost on the horse wrangler, who invariably sang the whole twelve verses through at one sitting:

We loved each other then, Lorena,
More than we ever dared to tell.
Oh, what we might have been, Lorena,
Had but our lovings prospered well.

Not only did Joe usually sing the whole twelve verses, but he lengthened them out by repeating as a refrain the last two lines to every verse, doing it in a melancholy, mysterious voice meant to express the deep, undying but hopeless passion that found its outlet only in song.

On one occasion, in the Bucket of Blood saloon in Holbrook, Arizona, Joe was boosted up onto the bar to sing "Lorena" to a bunch of hardened old cowpokes who had

158

drunk themselves into a maudlin state already. With the help of an impromptu barbershop quartet that joined in on his refrains, Joe soon had the whole bunch crying tears "as big as Mexican beans." As Joe's boss once observed, "Joe's an all right good singer, but the tune sort of scatters on him at times."[42] Although I'm a music-lover myself, I suspect, from this report, that I would have been of Rickety Bob's persuasion!

Not all cowboy songs were sad, like "Lorena" and "When the Work's All Done This Fall." Some were humorous, relating incidents that were fun to sing and hear. The very first book of cowboy songs, printed by Jack Thorp in 1908, had some songs that repeated the themes of the greenhorn being hoorawed, or the "educated feller" who turns out to be a top hand:

Educated Feller

We were camped upon the plains near the Cim-
    arron
When along came a stranger and stopped to
    argue some.
He was a well-educated feller, his talk just come
    in herds
And astonished all the punchers with his jaw-
    breaking words.

He had a well-worn saddle and we thought it
    kind'er strange
That he didn't know much about working on the
    range.
He'd been at work he said, up near the Santa Fe
And was cutting cross-country to strike the 7-D.
Had to quit an outfit up near Santa Fe;

159

Had some trouble with the boss, just what he
    didn't say.
Said his horse was 'bout give out and would like
    to get another
If the punchers wouldn't mind and it wasn't too
    much bother.

"Yes, we'll give you a horse, he's just as sound as
    a bun."
They quickly grabbed a lariat and roped the
    Zebra Dun,
Turned him over to the stranger
Then they waited to see the fun.

Old Dunny stands right still not seeming to
    know
Until the stranger's ready and a-fixing up to go.
When he goes into the saddle old Dunny leaves
    the earth;
He travels right straight up for all he was worth.

But he sits up in his saddle just pulling his mus-
    tache
Just like some summer boarder a-waiting for his
    hash.
Old Dunny pitched and bauled and had wall-
    eyed fits,
His hind feet perpendicular, his front ones in his
    bits.

With one foot in the stirrup, he just thought it
　　fun,
The other leg around the saddle horn the way
　　he rode old Dun.
He spurred him in the shoulder and hit him as
　　he whirled,
Just to show these flunky punchers the best
　　rider in the world.

The boss says to him, "You needn't go on
If you can use the rope like you rode old Dun.
You've a job with me if you want to come;
You're the man I've been looking for since the
　　year one."

"I can sling the rope, an' I'm not very slow;
I can catch nine times out of ten for any kind of
　　dough."
"Now there's one thing and a sure thing I've
　　learned since I was born:
That all these educated fellows are not green
　　horns."[43]

Thorp's printing of "Top Hand" takes a good look at the
cowboy who claims to be more than he is, who brags and
tells of his experiences, but "from the top to the bottom
he's a bold Jackass."[44] And his "Little Adobe Casa" on the
plains is like some line camps—crude cabins out on the
range where cowboys stay a week or a winter while looking after cattle:

161

The roof is ocateo,
The coyotes far and near.
The Greaser roams about the place all day.
Centipedes and Tarantulas
Crawl o'er as I sleep
In my little adobe casa on the plains.[45]

Now for some cowpokes, tarantulas were not all that fearful, although not entirely harmless; Philip Rollins tells of some cowboys who held tarantula duels:

Each of the huge, repulsive spiders which hopped about the bottom of a cracked soup-tureen carefully preserved for arena purposes, had financial backers amid the owners of the overhanging human faces. Occasionally a hairy gladiator ceased its cheery occupation of amputating its opponent's legs, jumped from the pit in which it belonged, and bit a spectator.[46]

Thorp's little book—it contained only twenty-four songs—even had a couple that described cowboy dances and other hilarity. One of them, "The Cowboy's Christmas Ball," had been collected via oral tradition (he says he got it from Miss Jessie Forbes of Eddy, New Mexico, present-day Carlsbad, in 1898). It was actually an accidentally garbled and deliberately localized version of Larry Chittenden's poem of the same name, probably learned for recitation purposes and passed around the southern New Mexico range orally because it described so well one of the chief recreations of the West. Its altered version, mentioning ranches and cowboys of the area, has considerable local interest.[47]

Another of the Western recreations—the only national sport to arise out of everyday work activities—is the rodeo. There too, in many well-worn stories, are bits of humor. The spirit and endurance of the cowboy and the cowgirl (remember, only the dead stay down) is almost proverbial, a fact that leads to a tale or two worth sharing. One has to do with a cowboy who took the dare to ride a tough horse. There was, however, a complicating factor:

This was just before election so there was four wagons that was camped right close together and they brought out beer, whiskey, and everything. We had an outlaw horse in the remuda of the Badger Pool I was with, so they'd been tryin' to get somebody to ride him. A young feller who had been drinkin' quite a lot said, "Rope me that pied horse," so they roped him and he saddled him up. I was ridin' a good horse and I knew something was gonna happen. I knew he was too drunk to get by with it, so when he got on him the horse made five or six jumps and throwed him off. Well, I caught him [the horse]. I said, "Well, Bob, get back on him. We'll try it again." He said, "Okay," so he got back on him. That time he broke the cinch and throwed him and the saddle and all. I said, "Well, when we get that cinch fixed we'll try him again." He said, "You know, I've sobered up enough that we ain't a gonna try him agin."[48]

And then there was a real rodeo, and Johnny Tulk was entered. It was just a little ole country rodeo in Yuma, Arizona, and Johnny figured he'd at least pick up some day money. Then he ran into Buck Ackeridge, Casey Tibbs, and Jim Shoulders—just about the best rodeoers in the business in those days—and they were entered too. As Johnny tells it,

I had to go on through with the deal, and I drew Tarbaby. Tarbaby's a pretty tough horse. The day before I drew a bare bronc and rode him out. He just jackrabbited all over around the arena like a rabbit jumpin' over mesquite bushes. So on the second day I had a saddle they wouldn't accept, so Casey Tibbs loaned me a saddle with the horn sawed off. So we'd have to grab a handful of dirt if we come off the horse; we couldn't find the saddle horn. I got in this committee saddle, and got all screwed down and this guy said, "Well, Pop, you better get your feet a little deeper in those stirrups." (It had ox bow stirrups.) I was afraid to jam my feet in there too far; I hadn't been on a bronc—a pitching saddle bronc—in five years. I got my hackamore string in my hand and they girded her up; he said, "Pop, you better get you another little grip on that hackamore string." I said, "Don't you worry about that, you just turn this horse loose." He said, "Well, it's your arm, Pop." So they turned him loose. Here come me and Tarbaby out; Tarbaby jumped up about three or four times in the air, just pitchin' like the devil and fell over backwards. He fell flat on his side. I had my left leg pinned under him; I was tryin' to kick my feet out of the stirrups, and I grabbed his ear, 'cause it looked like he was goin' to get up before I was sure I was free of things, and I wanted to be sure and have a good tight holt of him somewheres, so I said, "You son of a bitch!" This announcer just above me in the stands had a PA system, and he said, "This cowboy said the sun was sure shining bright on someone's beach." I heard him say that, and by that time I was about half mad; I thought he was makin' fun of me. I said, "Do I get a re-ride?" And he said, "Yes, you can have a re-ride, cowboy. You've got a re-ride coming." I thought I'd get a re-ride on a different horse, but they didn't even pull the saddle off him, they just pulled him down there and started back up there through the chutes, and I had to mount him again. And when I mounted him that time he came out of there, and I betcha if he jumped ten feet he jumped thirty feet across the ground before he ever hit the dirt, went straight up in the air, hit the ground two or three more times, and by that time I lost my balance, and I came off of him. This smart announcer up there on his PA system said, "Would you like another re-ride?" I said, "No sir, I have had all I want of that."[49]

The assortment of stories related to the everyday life of the cowboy is almost endless, but there is humor there to be shared—and sharing humor is at the heart of what keeps the cowboy going. Even a little story like one about the cowboy who gets so drunk he has trouble falling asleep is worth passing on:

Harry kept helping himself out of this barrel of Indian whiskey. Finally he stretched out and got ready to go to sleep, and he said to John, very solemn and careful, "John, will you do me a favor? Will you close my eyes for me?" He was so drunk he couldn't close his eyes. . . . A little thing like that was a big kick to us, you understand, a bunch of men out there by ourselves, with no newspapers or anything else to read, and nothing to do but get up and feed the stove.[50]

Not all cowboy humor is side-splitting, thigh-slapping, guffawing quality, but the everyday life of the cowpoke had its fun-filled moments; it traveled from camp to camp, saloon to saloon, and rodeo to rodeo, and it kept the boys sane. Reasonably sane, that is.

CHAPTER SEVEN

Cowboys Do the Damnedest Things

Sometimes, in the daily round of herding cattle, look-ing for screwworms in cows' hides, riding fence, greasing windmills, and cleaning out stock tanks, the cowboy's spirit simply has to break out. Even telling tall tales or playing pranks on others can't free the wild ones from the monotony of routine and responsibility. The direction such a "bust-out" may take is as varied as the many aspects of the cowboy's daily life—but it frequently is an enlargement upon what the cowboy does well. One of the first examples that comes to my mind is that memorable scene in Elmer Kelton's *The Good Old Boys* when Hewey Calloway and Snort Yarnell got even with the dude who was honking the horn on his ugly red automobile and scaring the horses:

Snort and Hewey looked each other in the eyes. Hewey saw the intention in Snort's face and concurred with a nod. Both unfastened their horn strings and shook loops into their ropes. Snort shouted, "I'll rope the head of the goddamn thing, Hewey. You come in there and heel it."

Spurring the roan horse, swinging the loop, Snort gave chase. One of the girls looked back, saw him and gasped. The dude looked over his shoulder, recognized Snort's intention and began trying for more speed. But the wagon road was rough and bouncy.

"Damn you, cowboy, don't you dare!" he shouted as Snort came up abreast of the vehicle. The roan was rolling its eyes and snorting in fear, but Snort kept spurring. In the final analysis, the horse feared Snort more than it feared the automobile.

Snort threw that great boxcar loop and landed a catch around the dashboard, one carbide lamp and a front wheel. He jerked up the slack and took a dally around his saddle horn. "Now heel it, Hewey!"

Hewey spurred Biscuit in, cast a quick loop over one of the rear wheels and rode south. Snort rode north.

The dude shook his fist. The girls grabbed hold of the seat and screamed.

As the two cowboys hit the ends of their ropes, they jerked the automobile half around and ran it into the ditch. The dude was thrown out over the dashboard.

Snort shouted, "We got it roped, but how do we hog-tie an automobile?"[1]

Well, they didn't tie up the automobile, but they did a pretty good job on the driver. Still, Snort's question is a good one, although others present themselves. The major one is not whether the dude needed to be given a lesson; it might more reasonably be, did the good old boys stop to think of the consequences of their actions? As a rule, good old boys of the cowboy persuasion do what comes to mind: Act first, think later, is a pretty standard rule.

And that standard rule—if it could be said to be a rule, with rule-busting cowpokes—is at the heart of a number of tales told about the doings of cowboys and cowgirls over the years. Take the story of High-Chin Bob, for example. If he had thought first—but then cowboys don't think first. They act first, think later, remember? As Jack Thorp printed the poem, apparently from the recitation or singing of someone who had read or heard Charles Badger Clark's original, it goes like this:

High-Chin Bob

Way up high in the Mokiones, among the mountain tops,
A lion cleaned a yearlin's bones and licked his thankful chops.
When who upon the scene should ride, a-trippin' down the slope,
But High-Chin Bob of sinful pride and maverick-hungry rope.

"Oh, Glory be to me!" says he, "an' fame's unfadin' flowers,
I ride my good top-hoss today and I'm top hand of the Lazy-J,
So Kitty cat, you're ours!"

The lion licked his paws so brown and dreamed
  soft dreams of veal,
As High-Chin's loop come circlin' down and
  roped him round his meal;
He yowled quick fury to the world and all the
  hills yelled back:
That top-hoss gave a snort and whirled and Bob
  caught up the slack.

"Oh, Glory be to me!" says he, "we'll hit the
  glory trail.
No man has looped a lion's head and lived to
  drag the bugger dead,
Till I shall tell the tale."

'Way up high in the Mokiones that top-hoss done
  his best
'Mid whippin' brush and rattlin' stones from can-
  yon-floor to crest;
Up and down and round and cross Bob pounded
  weak and wan,
But pride still glued him to the hoss and glory
  drove him on.

"Oh, Glory be to me," says he, "this glory trail is
  rough,
I'll keep this dally round the horn until the toot
  of judgment morn,
Before I'll holler 'nough!"

Three suns had rode their circle home beyond
   the desert rim
And turned their star herds loose to roam the
   ranges high and dim,
And whenever Bob turned and hoped the limp
   remains to find,
A red-eyed lion, belly roped, but healthy, loped
   behind!

"Oh, Glory be to me," says Bob, "he kain't be
   drug to death!
These heroes that I've read about were only
   fools that stuck it out
To the end of mortal breath!"

'Way up high in the Mokiones, if you ever come
   there at night,
You'll hear a ruckus amongst the stones that'll
   lift your hair with fright;
You'll see a cow-hoss thunder by and a lion trail
   along,
And the rider bold, with chin on high, sings
   forth his glory song;

"Oh, Glory be to me!" says he, "and to my
   mighty noose!
Oh pardner, tell my friends below I took a ragin'
   dream in tow,
And if I didn't lay him low,—I never turned him
   loose!"[2]

171

Old High-Chin Bob is fictional, of course, but many a real-life cowboy and cowgirl has "taken a ragin' dream in tow"—and sometimes they, too, couldn't turn it loose. It hasn't always been something like a mountain lion—but sometimes it has been.

Curt Brummett has a story that fits into this category, in a general sort of way. And it also fits into the concept of acting first, thinking later. I can't vouch for Curt's veracity; I don't know if he tells the truth even occasionally. But he does tell a good tale.

Stovepipes
BY CURT BRUMMETT

Going to school in eastern New Mexico can at times be as dangerous as preg-testing mountain lions in their native habitat. And there has been a time or two when even getting home from school was a very definite act of survival.

My brothers and I rode horses to school about ninety percent of the time (when we went to school), and the other ten percent, when our sister happened to be around, we would have to take the wagon. She just didn't like to be a-horseback.

From the time we left our place until we got to the schoolhouse, we would grow in numbers. Some kids would be riding burros, others horses, and sometimes a mule or two would be present. I always wondered what such a group of people would look like coming out of the hills and swarming down on the schoolhouse. Thinking back, I bet it was quite a comical sight.

The older boys made a little extra money by breaking horses for other ranches, and what better way is there to break a horse than to ride 'im eighteen miles a day, and expose him to civilization or a reasonable facsimile?

Now goin' to school was not the most enjoyable part of our lives, and even though we tolerated it, we didn't really enjoy it all that much. And adding to the unenjoyable part was that three miles from school we had to pick up our teacher, Mr. Slimtech. Slimtech rode an eight-year-old mule he bought from our dad. Now this mule was goofy as a drunk chicken and not near as reliable. Dad told old Slimtech that the mule wasn't to be trusted, but the teacher wanted that mule and he bought him. And, till one or two unplanned events took place, the teacher and the mule got along fine.

Every day all of us kids would come down the trail and you could hear lunch pails rattlin' against saddles and kids talkin' and laughin'; then Mr. Slimtech would ride out on Lucifer and all the joy came to a halt. We noticed, too, that Slimtech's lunch bucket never rattled after that first day he rode Lucifer to school. It seemed that Lucifer didn't appreciate being used as a pack mule to haul noisy lunch buckets.

Slimtech noticed that we all had our lunch buckets tied to the saddle strings, so he thought he'd do things our way. We watched as Slimtech tied his lunch bucket to the saddle and as he mounted old Lucifer. From there on things got pretty entertainin'. As soon as old Lucifer noticed a strange sound comin' from his left shoulder, he sold out. He swallowed his head, jumped high and hard to the right, and at the same time tried to kick that lunch bucket out of the country. Not bein' able to get this done, he pulled a stampede. He might not have gone quite as crazy if Slimtech hadn't screamed like a gut-shot panther.

My brother, realizin' that Slimtech wasn't any part of a horseman or a muleteer, quickly spurred his bronc and tried to catch old Lucifer and the schoolteacher. The last thing we saw of them was a runaway mule, one very scared (I should say terrified) schoolteacher, and my older brother tryin' to fix a rope on one of 'em. And they went out of sight down a shallow canyon.

School finally got started about three hours later than usual. Old Slimtech couldn't decide whether or not Joe missed those first six loops on purpose or not. Joe was considered to be the best roper for quite a ways, and old Slimtech figured he mighta missed those loops just so's he could chase 'em all over those hills. But even though he didn't want to admit it, he was tickled pink that the seventh loop had caught old Lucifer.

Of course, this minor display of action set a couple of idle minds to turnin'. Between Slimtech's place and the schoolhouse there was a cabin, with a stovepipe, that just happened to be very close to the trail. In fact, the wall wasn't but two or three feet from the edge of the road.

The mornin' just before Christmas vacation there was a very special feeling in the mornin' air. Each kid in our little ragtag cavalry, from the youngest to the oldest, was feelin' the holiday spirit. Each was makin' jokes and laughin' at all of the others. Even when Mr. Slimtech joined the group, not even he could kill the cheerful spirit

we had goin'. But before he got to school that
mornin' he would want to kill each one of us.
Maybe not the younger ones, because they
could still be taught right from left. But anyone
over seven would have to go.

Tom and Joe were ridin' broncs and they were
havin' quite a time showin' off for the rest of us.
They would break from the group and race to a
jack pine and then stampede back to the group
screamin' like chargin' Apaches, all this to the
delight of us younger kids. Especially me. I idol-
ized those two for their ability to ride and rope.
And I longed for the day when I could ride those
green-broke mountain horses to school instead
of the more settled ranch horses. Little did I
know that my settled old ranch horse was goin'
to be the one to cause just one more delay in
the educational process of our great nation.

It had to be his fault. 'Cause if he hadn't gone
so close to that old abandoned cabin I would
never have had the chance to rope that stovepipe. As the group came close to the buildin' old
Slimtech had made the older boys calm down
and ride beside him at the head of the group.
His excuse was that they was scarin' the other
children with their wild and reckless actions.
Actually old Lucifer was actin' like he wanted to
join the fun, and old Slimtech didn't feel like
bein' chased all over the country by a seven-
teen-year-old maniac swingin' a rope. So the
boys calmed down and rode in beside old killjoy.

While the boys were showin' off and bein'
called down I was playin' with my catch rope. I
had been wantin' to show off a little myself, but
since there wasn't any maverick bulls or wild

black stallions to capture, I did my act simply by ropin' the stovepipe on that old cabin.

As soon as I turned that rope loose I had a very strange feelin' that I done messed up. Boy! Talk about a right feelin'. At that same instant I started tryin' to figure out how I was goin' to get my rope back. Boy, was I silly. I found out in the next three or four seconds that gettin' that rope back was gonna be a damn sight simpler than gettin' all them other little problems straightened out.

Before I could get my horse stopped and ask for help, the sound of that whaleline scrapin' on that rusty pipe had already spooked 'im. The rope tightened, makin' the pipe really squeak. Now all that noise plus a tight rope attracted attention. My horse pulled a one-critter stampede. And everybody saw it but old Slimtech and Lucifer. They didn't need to see it, 'cause in about two seconds they was part of it.

I sure never thought that old horse could pull down a whole buildin'. But he did. When the boards started breakin', horses started leavin', kids started screamin', burros started brayin', and even the dogs started barkin' in the road. When we finally got to the end of any movin' parts, that old horse just kept on goin'. He was tryin' to buck and run away all at the same time, and each time he hit the end of the rope it just kinda stalled him out. After about twice the stovepipe came loose; it passed us like a bullet.

By now any critter that could run was doin' so. And my old horse, not wantin' to be left alone with a renegade stovepipe on the loose, figured he'd better catch up with the others.

Since him and old Lucifer had run together in the same pastures he just naturally figured they should run down the road together. And he proceeded to catch up—or try to catch up.

It is extremely hard to run from somethin' that is tied to you. And I might add purt near impossible to escape it. But as we caught up to Lucifer and Slimtech, that old stovepipe took a bounce for the worse. Old Lucifer had figured out that my horse was the one the stovepipe was after, so he slowed down just a hair. At this same time the stovepipe came off my rope and bounced right into Lucifer's rear end. Lucifer gained some ground.

Seems like one of the guy wires on the stovepipe snagged in the mule's tail. As Slimtech and Lucifer passed through town and crossed the river some people heard Slimtech holler somethin' about justifiable homicide, between terror-filled screams.

It only took about three hours to regroup and gather up all the loose kids and horses and burros. Tom had bucked off right at the start of this mess, and Joe's horse had stampeded off towards the river, but they were back and laughin'. So I knew they weren't goin' to kill me. But I still had to face old Slimtech.

About three in the afternoon Old Slimtech and Lucifer came to school. Both looked like someone had poured a sack full of bobcats on 'em. He was so glad to be alive that he wasn't even goin' to punish me—yet. He said, the way he figured it, if it hadn't been for those two cowboys runnin' him down, he would have been to Fort Sumner by four o'clock.

177

He dismissed what was left of the class and we headed home. Everyone was ridin' just like always, except Slimtech. When I asked 'im how come he was walkin' and leadin' old Lucifer, he just glared at me. And when I tried to show 'im how really sorry I was by offerin' to let 'im ride double with me, he just kinda went blank. That's when I rode off and left him and Lucifer, him talkin' to Lucifer about some kind of conspiracy, and Lucifer agreein' with 'im.

I might add that for several weeks after the renegade stovepipe trick we had a little trouble gettin' our horses and burros past that old abandoned cabin—at least the ones that had witnessed it throwin' that stovepipe at me and old Slimtech.[3]

Brummett's is the only tale I've run into of somebody lassoing a stovepipe, but the tales are full of folks roping other varmints. In addition to that cowgirl I mentioned in the introduction—the one who lassoed a Mexican lion and (unlike High-Chin Bob) dragged him all the way home— several other reports of fearsome roping targets can be discussed.

Bears seem to be pretty popular among the crazy cowboy coterie. Barbara Fox tells a grisly tale along this line:

My brother and I roped a bear one day. We run him all over the country, up my dad's homestead there. He was pretty well tired time we caught him, but we both had our ropes on him a number of times. Then my brother broke his rope, so naturally he borrowed sister's. But at

the time we could either one of us roped him,
he was pretty tired.

My brother got the rope around his neck and
dallied the rope around a buck fence post. We
weren't too far from a buck fence. I held the
bear and he got an ax. Killed him with an ax. I
do think I come as near choking him to death as
my brother did to killing him.[4]

The picture accompanying this account shows that this
was no teddy bear—it was a full-grown one, and Barbara
and her brother look to be around ten and eleven, respectively. I guess you wouldn't expect such young'uns to have
acquired too much judgment by that age.

There are tall tales, of course, about bear-ropings, but
Joyce Roach tells for truth the story of Ann Henderson
who grew up in Butch Cassidy country. She once "roped a
bear cub and barely missed death when the mama bear
made a swipe at Ann and broke her horse's neck instead."[5]

John Young, the source of J. Frank Dobie's *A Vaquero of
the Brush Country,* told Dobie of a number of roping adventures. Once, in Colorado while hunting cattle, Young and
John Duncan came upon a herd of elk and Young lassoed
one:

He was bounding along with great leaps and
at the instant he reached the end of the rope
was in midair. The jerk whirled him around and
he hit the ground flat. He bounced to his feet
like a rubber ball and ran on the rope again, but
this time I did not throw him. I could see that he
was getting mad. He quit running; his hair stood
straight up; he looked at me viciously for a few

seconds; then he shook his head and came straight for me. I realized that I must either cut the rope and move or else shoot him. I did not want to lose my rope. I reached for my six-shooter and already had it out of the holster when I heard Duncan yell. He had made a run and had roped the charging elk by the hind legs. We had no desire to kill him, but we had to throw him down in order to take my rope off him. We tied him in such a way that we could loosen him from a mounted position. When he got up he had blood in his eye, and right there we had to do some tall riding before he got his mind again on freedom and the open spaces.[6]

And these were grown men, playing! Young also shared stories with Dobie of roping bears, buck deer, buffalo calves, bobcats, and other critters—and may have even tried his rope on a razorback hog, a tough item to rope, because "this creature holds its nose so close to the earth that, except on open ground where the vegetation is low, it is almost impossible to get a noose over its head."[7]

Ramon Adams tells the tale of Bill Bullard, who had a stirring adventure

ropin' two wolves, half dead from poison, and tryin' to bring 'em to camp on hossback, one on each end of his rope. His hoss went "hog-wild" when he saw those two wolves so close, and he didn't slow down when he reached camp. Bill was welcomed with such sarcasm as, "What's your hurry, Bill, won't you stay to eat?" "Don't hurry, Bill, you got lots of time," "If you're going

180

to Medicine Hat, a little more to the left." Bill had maybe heard of killin' two birds with one stone, but he learned to never rope two any-things with one rope.[8]

Roping animals is one thing; and roping an automobile to teach the driver a lesson is another. But what can be said for the rope-happy cowpoke who builds a loop for a rail-road engine? Paul Patterson snitches on Lee Reynolds, Cow Boy, one of the greatest natural wits Paul ever ran into:

> Up in Odessa one time, what with Lee feeling his corn (distilled, cowboy equivalent of his oats), he had Old Rowdy girted up tight, a siz-able loop built, and was waitin' for the T&P pas-senger train to pull in—or out. Either way he was going to rope the smokestack.
>
> "Lee," pleaded one of the "Clabber Hill" hands, "don't do it. You don't know what you're a-ropin'!"
>
> "Ahhhh. No, and they don't know what I'm ridin' either."[9]

Paul didn't report whether Lee actually roped the T&P or not, but John Young says that

> one time at Cotulla, on the Nueces River, a va-quero who was a little braver for liquor roped the smokestack of an engine that was moving towards Laredo at the rate of twenty miles an

hour. The rope was strong and so was the engine. After the engineer stopped the train and the cowboy got himself and his horse separated from the property belonging to the I&GN Railroad Company, he was thoroughly sober.[10]

And Philip Rollins, who was recording the doings of the cowboy over half a century ago, said that "if certain records be accurate, more than one white man and many an Indian quickly passed to the Happy Hunting Ground, jerked thither by a reata caught about the smokestack of a moving locomotive."[11] Had he been asked, I'm sure Rollins would have agreed that cowboys do the damnedest things!

Another method of bringing one's quarry to the ground may well have started out as a prank, but it did not involve a rope. Nonetheless, with certain variations, it may have given a new surge of life to a special brand of action in the rodeo arena, and one of the most popular—steer wrestling or bulldogging.

Bill Pickett, a young black cowboy-to-be, had noticed that a catch dog could bring an animal much larger than himself to the ground by grabbing the upper lip of the animal with his teeth. So Bill tried the same trick, first on a calf, and it worked. He grabbed the calf by the ears, and then "Bill fastened his teeth on the calf's upper lip, turned loose of its ears, and with a flip of his body, threw it to the ground." Days later, on his way to school, Bill passed a bunch of cowboys branding calves, and he bragged to the boys of his newfound ability. The cowboys didn't believe him, but they let him try, expecting to see a bit of action and a put-down of an uppity youngster. They lassoed a good-sized calf and let Bill do the holding while they did the branding.

Bill carefully got his bulldog hold and waved the cowboys to turn the calf loose, which they were eager to do in order that the show might start. Much to their surprise, the calf scarcely made a sound or moved a muscle as the hot branding iron was applied to its tender hide. Given the signal to turn loose, Bill let go and the animal scrambled to its feet and ran off to join the other calves. The cowboys were amazed and soon spread the word around Austin that the Pickett kid could bulldog a calf while it was being branded. Thus began a legend that was to grow into one of the most colorful realities of the sports world in the twentieth century.[12]

From this beginning Pickett learned to bulldog full-sized steers by using his teeth, leaping from the back of a horse and bringing them to the ground in record time. On a bet he even did the feat with both hands tied behind his back! For many years he was a stellar attraction in the famous Miller Brothers' 101 Wild West Show, and in 1971 he was elected posthumously to the National Cowboy Hall of Fame, the first black cowboy to be so honored.[13]

Many of the wild actions of the cowboy are less showy, but they are worth recalling. One has to do with that ever-able provoker of damphoolishness, looking at the world with a whiskey bottle for a telescope. During Prohibition, when a doctor's prescription was needed to get whiskey legally, Bud Colbaugh "had the good fortune to get bit by a rattlesnake." Eventually, however, he got well.

Even so, he kept going back for more medicine, but the doctor kept turning him down.

Early one morning a neighbor noticed Bud out
at the woodpile juggling mesquite around to
beat the band.

"Bud, I know you better'n that. You ain't about
to cut no wood."

"Oh, hell no!"

"Then what're ye up to?"

"I'm looking fer me another snake."[14]

With Prohibition over, the need for a personal snake was less vital, but the results of over-imbibing could still produce striking results.

Dick Robbins, oldtime rodeo hand, was holed
up in a hotel room with some fellow contestants.
The boys were celebrating with liquid refresh-
ments . . . . This particular evenin' one ol' boy,
quite likkered up, declared he could jump out of
the window and fly around the building. The
bets were on. The performer staggered to the
open window, waved his arms toward the heav-
ens—and jumped. Landing in the bushes below
sobered him. Wobbling dazed back into the
room, he attacked his partner's loyalty with,
"Why'd you let me do that?" His partner hic-
cupped and explained, "I thought you could do
it. I lost ten dollars on you."[15]

No liquor, no wild animal roping, and not even any bulldogging of steers with the teeth is involved in this next and last item, but the reader must agree that it qualifies for the finals in the "damnedest things" competition, even though the desired result was beneficial rather than just cowboy craziness. A young fellow named George Clutch had alienated himself from his family with his wild, unpredictable ways. They actually ran him off from home. After several years working on ranches in the Greenbelt area of Texas, he had settled down and married a lovely girl, and soon they had a darling baby daughter. He wanted to share his new condition with his folks, but he got word they didn't even open his letters.

George finally hit upon a plan. He made a compact with the undertaker. He got the undertaker to send his parents a formal invitation to their son's funeral. His trick worked; in a few days his entire family—father, mother, brothers, and sister—dressed in mourners' black, got off the train in Childress. A person can imagine their consternation when the first person to meet them was their son. His father, realizing his ingenuity, burst into gales of laughter, embraced George, blessed the beautiful wife and daughter, and reestablished friendly relations with the George Clutch family.[16]

Although the consequences of George's trick were positive, one can imagine that they could have been quite painful; the soul-searching of his parents, their wondering, "If only we'd . . . ." Still, I don't reckon I can top it—unless High-Chin Bob were to come lopin' through with two mountain lions—one on each end of his rope. And I don't imagine that'll happen anytime soon.

Afterword

"When you come to the end of a perfect day, and you sit alone with your thoughts . . . ." That old song kept running through my mind as this book came to a close. Among those thoughts was just how much fun the whole trip has been.

Rereading old familiar books, rediscovering stories I had long forgotten; finding new accounts of cowboy fun and foolishness; leaning on friends, old and new—all these memories come back to mind as I relax for a moment.

Elmer Kelton, who grew up a cowboy and writes with inside knowledge, encouraged me a lot, and gave me permission to use long passages from his *Good Old Boys,* which is truly a classic. Had I not talked with Elmer about my project, I never would have met Curt Brummett, who can flat tell a humorous story with just the right touch; he does right well, for an old cowboy. And his kindness in letting me publish some of his "children"—well, that was like the generosity of the Old West. I'm hoping this book helps bring him an audience for books of his own that he wants to write. Paul Patterson was a cowboy in his younger days, as well as Elmer's English teacher, and he has a style all his own—plus a generous heart.

John Erickson, when I asked him for permission to use some of his work, wrote back he'd be pleased to let me, and saying, "I would be even pleaseder if there were some money involved in the exchange, seeing as how I am trying to support a wife, three hungry kids, a dog, a cat, and a bird with my writing. But since you didn't mention wages, I presume this is one of them deals to help out the neighbors." Well, it is, and he did, and I'm grateful, and I hope that folks will go after more of his work than the little sample included here. He's written a bunch of great books!

Also, Joyce Gibson Roach helped me see what a valuable place the cowgirl filled in the Old West. And C.L. "Doc" Sonnichsen, an authority on Western humor and fiction as well, was always ready with a quip or a suggestion.

The title of the last chapter, as well as the cover picture idea, came from my memory of High-Chin Bob, introduced to me nearly forty years ago by Everett Gillis. I shared the poem with my *amigo* José Cisneros (who had also done the cover for my *Mexican-American Folklore*), and the resulting cover for this book is dear to my heart, as José is. I wrote the biography/introduction for his *Riders Across the Centuries,* which won the Wrangler Award from the Cowboy Hall of Fame, quite deservedly. And, not having a real cowboy background myself, I found it was mighty handy to be able to pick up the telephone when I hit a snag and ask my friend, colleague, and former student, Deane Mansfield-Kelley, what "Three wraps and a hooey" was—or a dozen other bits of cowboy lingo. (That's how a waddie hogties what he has roped: he wraps the piggin' string around three hooves three times, then pulls it between two hooves—that's the hooey, if you didn't know.) She was a teenage cowgirl herself, and knows the ropes.

The August House folks are good to work with, and I

hope this is not our last venture together. They are long-suffering, and put up with a lot from me. But without them—and the daily help and encouragement of my wife and helpmeet, Lucy Fischer West—this work would not be. I even had to sneak and wash the dishes from time to time, Lucy was so protective of me and insistent on freeing me from distracting labors. But I had to keep my hand in.

Still, the bottom line is that the cowboys who over the years managed to live with the dust and the bone-weary days in the saddle, their ability to get up from having been stood on their heads by some fractious bronc and laugh about it, and their willingness to frolic when the time was right—those cowboys made this work possible. I'll be forever grateful that they lived and laughed and shared with us. A bunch of 'em have gone up the Long Trail, but their memories linger on, ¡*gracias a Dios!*

Notes

Introduction

[1]John I. White, *Git Along Little Dogies: Songs and Songmakers of the American West* (Urbana: University of Illinois Press, 1975), pp. 193-95, gives the name of the dead cowboy as Charlie—which sometimes scans and sometimes doesn't. When I read his version, I was impressed with the accuracy of my memory after more than half a century.

[2]N. Howard Thorp, *Songs of the Cowboys* (Estancia, New Mexico: News Print Shop, 1908), pp. 9-10; see also John O. West, "Jack Thorp and John A. Lomax: Oral or Written Transmission?" *Western Folklore* 26.2 (April 1967): 113-18.

[3]John Steinbeck, *Tortilla Flat* (New York: Viking, 1963), pp. 137-38.

[4]John A. Lomax, *Cowboy Songs and Other Frontier Ballads* (New York: Macmillan, 1920), p. 149.

[5]Booth Tarkington, *Penrod* (New York: Grossett and Dunlap, 1914), pp. 10-11.

[6]John O. West, "Billy the Kid: Hired Gun or Hero?" *The Sunny Slopes of Long Ago* (Dallas: Southern Methodist University Press, 1966), Publications of the Texas Folklore Society 33: 70-80.

[7]Mody C. Boatright, class lectures, "Southwestern Life and Literature," The University of Texas, June 1962.

[8]Glenn Ohrlin, *The Hell-Bound Train: A Cowboy Songbook* (Urbana: University of Illinois Press, 1973), pp. 73-79.

[9]C.L. Sonnichsen, *The Laughing West* (Athens, Ohio: Swallow Press/Ohio University Press, 1988), p. 5.

[10]Nora Ramírez, "Humor in Cattle Country," unpublished manuscript in the University of Texas at El Paso Folklore Archive.

[11]Paul Patterson, "Cowboy Comedians and Horseback Humorists," *The Golden Log* (Dallas: Southern Methodist University Press, 1962), Publications of the Texas Folklore Society 31: 106.

[12]John C. Duval, *The Adventures of Big-Foot Wallace, the Texas Ranger and Hunter* (Macon, Georgia: J.W. Burke, 1870), pp. 293-94. The confusion of the name of the tarantella, a whirling dance "once thought to be a remedy for tarantism" *(American Heritage Dictionary)* with the hairy spider of the Southwest is evidence of Duval's— or Wallace's—breadth of knowledge and lore.

[13]Elmer Kelton, *The Good Old Boys* (rpt. Fort Worth: Texas Christian University Press, 1985), p. 250.

[14]John R. Erickson, *Cowboys Are Partly Human* (Perryton, Texas: Maverick Books, 1983), p. 16.

[15]Collected by the author from a rodeo cowboy in Odessa, Texas, in 1960, and heard all over the Southwest.

[16]Lora Shawver and Walt Cousins, *Chuck Wagon Windies and Range Poems* (San Antonio: Naylor, 1934), p. 30.

[17]"Texas Girl Captures Lion with Lasso," undated clipping from unnamed newspaper in the Western History Collection, Denver Public Library, cited in Joyce Gibson Roach, *The Cowgirls* (Houston: Cordovan Corp., 1978), p. 31.

Chapter One. The Cowboy Talks Funny

[1]Kelton, *Good Old Boys,* pp. 184-86.

[2]Kelton, *Good Old Boys,* pp. 91-95. Of the dog incident, Mr. Kelton wrote, "I based it loosely on a story told to me by Elton Mims of Water Valley, Texas. His father, Uncle Bob Mims, was supposed to have pulled a similar trick on somebody years ago. Uncle Bob was an early-day wagon boss in this country, as well as a steer roper." Letter to the author, January 18, 1989.

[3]Ramírez, "Humor in Cattle Country." Ramon F. Adams, in *The Old-Time Cowhand* (New York: Macmillan, 1961), pp. 39-40, says, "While much of the cowboy's language needed some expurgatin' for parlor use, he didn't depend on smutty stories for his taletellin' like so many of the stories the city man tells; nor did sex enter into the subjects he discussed or joked about. In the early days women were

too scarce to be looked upon except with respect and admiration. There were only two kinds, good and bad, and the good were put on a pedestal while the bad were uncondemned."

[4]Bill Walton Flynt, the author's brother-in-law, had a wealth of such stories. He told this story to the author around 1936.

[5]J. Frank Dobie, *A Vaquero of the Brush Country* (Boston: Little, Brown, 1943), p. 34.

[6]Personal interviews by the author with Paul Patterson and Elmer Kelton, Uvalde, Texas, 23 March 1989.

[7]J. Frank Dobie, "Mustang Gray: Fact, Tradition, and Song," in *Tone the Bell Easy* (Dallas: Southern Methodist University Press, 1932), Publications of the Texas Folklore Society 10: 109-11.

[8]Lawrence Clayton, "The Mounted Herdsmen of the West: Regional Variation—the Vaquero, Cowboy, and Buckaroo," unpublished manuscript.

[9]Paul Patterson, *Crazy Women in the Rafters: Memories of a Texas Boyhood* (Norman: University of Oklahoma Press, 1976), p. 36.

[10]John O. West, "The Galloping Gourmet, or The Chuck Wagon Cook and His Craft," in *By Land and Sea: Studies in the Folklore of Work and Leisure,* ed. Roger D. Abrahams, Kenneth S. Goldstein, and Wayland D. Hand (Hatboro, Pennsylvania: Legacy Books, 1985), p. 221.

[11]Mody C. Boatright, *Folk Laughter on the American Frontier* (New York: Collier Books, 1961), p. 160.

[12]John J. Baker, "Fort Worth Texas Narrative," Fort Worth History Notes, Folder 68: Interviews, Texas Writers Project, Barker History Center, The University of Texas at Austin, 26830, cited in West, "Galloping Gourmet," p. 221.

[13]Philip A. Rollins, *The Cowboy* (New York: Charles Scribner's Sons, 1922), p. 77.

[14]Ramon Adams, *Come and Get It: The Story of the Old Cowboy Cook* (Norman: University of Oklahoma Press, 1952), p. 111, cited in West, "Galloping Gourmet," p. 221.

[15]West, "Galloping Gourmet," p. 221.

[16]Adams, *Come and Get It,* pp. 91-92, cited in West, "Galloping Gourmet," p. 221. See also Tommy J. Boley, ed., *An Autobiography of a West Texas Pioneer, Ella Elgar Bird Dumont* (Austin: University of Texas Press, 1988), p. 61. Mrs. Dumont recalls the dish's being called "'County Attorney' in the presence of ladies and children, as the real name like some of the horses' names would not look well in print."

[17]Boatright, *Folk Laughter,* p. 161.

[18]John R. Erickson, "Language of the Cow Camp Has Flavor All Its Own," *Prorodeo Sports News* (27 June 1979): 23-24.

[19]Patterson, *Crazy Women,* p. 99.

[20]Patterson, *Crazy Women,* p. 105.

[21]Will S. James, *27 Years a Mavrick, or Life on the Texas Range* (rpt. Austin: Steck-Vaughn Co., 1968), p. 168. I have normalized the punctuation.

[22]Paul Patterson, "The Cowboy's Code," *The Sunny Slopes of Long Ago* (Dallas: Southern Methodist University Press, 1966), Publications of the Texas Folklore Society 33: 42-44.

[23]Dobie, *Vaquero,* p. 273.

[24]James, *27 Years,* p. 163.

[25]Paul Patterson, *Pecos Tales* (Austin: Texas Folklore Society, 1967), p. 36.

Chapter Two. Tall Tales

[1]Boatright, *Folk Laughter,* pp. 99-101. Don Dedera, in *The Cactus Sandwich and Other Tall Tales of the Southwest* (Flagstaff, Arizona: Northland Press, 1986), pp. 55-56, recounts the same basic tale by John Hance; his horse jumped into the canyon too, falling 3,000 feet—but John jumped off and had only three feet to fall. To the open-mouthed tourists listening to his tale, he often admitted, "We were both killed."

[2]J. Frank Dobie, *The Longhorns* (New York: Bramhall House, 1941), p. 84.

[3]Personal interview with Ronnie Anderson, 27 January 1989, in El Paso; Mr. Anderson, born on a Colorado ranch, has cowboyed all over Texas, New Mexico, Arizona, Colorado, and Montana. Like Mark Twain, he tells the truth, mainly. Everett Gillis, in "Weather Talk from the Caprock," *Folk Travelers* (Dallas: Southern Methodist University Press, 1953), Publications of the Texas Folklore Society 25: 200, also reports the log chain wind indicator. Dedera, *Cactus Sandwich,* p. 10, tells of a man no-billed for shooting his neighbor; the neighbor had put up a windmill where there wasn't enough breeze to run a second one.

[4]Paul Patterson, *Sam Magoo and Texas Too* (Dallas: Mathis, Van Nort, & Co., 1947), p. 49. Doubtless the well would have been even shallower had Willie not been wearing high-heeled boots.

[5]Anderson interview.

[6]C.L. Sonnichsen, *Cowboys and Cattle Kings: Life on the Range Today* (rpt. Westport, Connecticut: Greenwood Press, 1980), p. 70.

[7]Patterson, *Sam Magoo,* p. 43. We dwellers in West Texas, especially during the drought that produced the Dust Bowl, often had to defend the wild weather we "enjoyed." But there were advantages too: Over in Sam Magoo's Pecos country Willie Wilson's mother used to stand on her porch during spring dust storms when she wanted a change of scenery; from there she could "watch county after county blow by," p. 48.

[8]I first heard this story about 1935; since then I have often heard it and seen it in print in one form or another. It's too good a story to leave untold!

[9]Boatright, *Folk Laughter,* p. 90.

[10]Mody Boatright, *Tall Tales from Texas Cow Camps* (rpt. Dallas: Southern Methodist University Press, 1982), pp. 83-86.

[11]Boatright, *Tall Tales,* pp. 89-90.

[12]Boatright, *Tall Tales,* pp. 92-94; Dedera, *Cactus Sandwich,* p. 53, tells how John Hance's wife died: "Broke her leg. Had to shoot her."

[13]"Pecos Bill," in *Melody Time* (Walt Disney Productions, about 1954).

[14]Martha Faye Handley Lee, "Legends and Folklore of the Greenbelt of the Texas Panhandle" (master's thesis, The University of Texas at El Paso, 1969), p. 114.

[15]Shawver and Cousins, *Chuck Wagon Windies,* pp. 183-84.

[16]Stanley W. Harris, "Stories of Ranch People," *Singers and Storytellers* (Dallas: Southern Methodist University Press, 1961), Publications of the Texas Folklore Society 30: 176.

[17]*Folk Tales from the Patagonia Area, Santa Cruz County, Arizona,* University of Arizona Bulletin, General Bulletin No. 13, 19: 4 (October 1948), quoted in Benjamin A. Botkin, *A Treasury of Western Folklore* (New York: Crown, 1951), p. 672.

[18]Patterson, *Sam Magco,* pp. 40-41.

[19]Lee, p. 102.

[20]Roy Scudday, "The Musical Snake," *From Hell to Breakfast* (Dallas: Southern Methodist University Press, 1944), Publications of the Texas Folklore Society 19: 162-64; also quoted in Botkin, *Western Folklore,* p. 672.

[21]J. Frank Dobie, *Rattlesnakes* (rpt. Austin: University of Texas Press, 1982), pp. 39-40.

[22]Joe Evans, *A Corral Full of Stories* (El Paso: McMath, 1939), p. 49; also quoted in Botkin, *Western Folklore,* p. 672. Patterson, in "Cow-

boy Comedians," has a similar tale about Snaky Price, who says "if he hadn't beat the dam thang to a rough header he reckon the bear'd a roped him and drug him slap to death!"

[23]Shawver and Cousins, *Chuck Wagon Windies,*pp. 184-85.

[24]Patterson, *Pecos Tales,* p. 14.

[25]Boatright, *Tall Tales,* pp. 104-5. Dedera, *Cactus Sandwich,* has a story about some gifted dogs: one liked to herd quail, stuffing them down a prairie dog hole and covering it with his paw, letting them fly one at a time so his master could shoot them, pp. 53-54; others learned to throw and hold a calf, then brand and earmark it; later they got so haughty they wanted to do the roping, letting the man brand the calves, pp. 87-88.

Chapter Three. The Cowboy's Pranks

[1]Rollins, *The Cowboy,* pp. 44-46.

[2]James, *27 Years,* pp. 133-34.

[3]Rollins, *The Cowboy,* pp. 184-86.

[4]James, *27 Years,* pp. 136-38.

[5]James, *27 Years,* pp. 55-60; I normalized the punctuation somewhat.

[6]Bart McDowell, *The American Cowboy in Life and Legend* (Washington, D.C.: National Geographic Society, 1972), p. 25.

[7]J. Marvin Hunter, ed., *The Trail Drivers of Texas* (n.p.: The Old Trail Drivers Association, 1920), pp. 115-16.

[8]Dobie, *Vaquero,* 158-59.

[9]Hunter, *Trail Drivers,* pp. 487-88.

[10]James B. Gillett, *Six Years with the Texas Rangers* (rpt. Lincoln: University of Nebraska Press, 1976), p. 54. E.C. Abbott, *We Pointed Them North* (rpt. Norman: University of Oklahoma Press, 1955), p. 202, note 1, records: "Conley kicked all night because the tent leaked on his face some men are never satisfied. This morning I blew the boys up with Black Powder (threw some of it on the fire) it created a little commotion."

[11]McDowell, *American Cowboy,* pp. 38-39.

[12]Patterson, "Cowboy Comedians," pp. 105-6.

[13]Shawver and Cousins, *Chuck Wagon Windies,* pp. 148-51.

[14]Ramírez, "Humor in Cattle Country," p. 19.

[15]Erickson, *Cowboys Are Partly Human,* p. 68.

[16]Ramírez, "Humor in Cattle Country," p. 18.

[17]Ramírez, "Humor in Cattle Country," p. 17.

[18]Dobie, *Vaquero*, p. 88-89.

[19]Owen Wister, *The Virginian* (New York: Macmillan, 1902), pp. 113-22. James D. Bratcher's "The Baby-Switching Story," *The Sunny Slopes of Long Ago* (Dallas: Southern Methodist University Press, 1966), Publications of the Texas Folklore Society 33: 110-17, not only traces the likely sources of Wister's story, but demonstrates the popularity of the folktale behind it.

[20]Guy Logsdon, "The Cowboy Dance: From Ranch House to Road House," unpublished manuscript, pp. 23-28. Logsdon, renowned authority on cowboy music and dance, has a rich collection of bawdy cowboy songs—"the ones they really sang"—due out in August 1989, in *The Whorehouse Bells Are Ringing* (Urbana: University of Illinois Press). He assures me it is absolutely unexpurgated; I cain't hardly wait!

[21]Patterson, *Crazy Women*, p. 70.

[22]The game of 42, which Mr. Hoyle seems never to have heard of, is a bridge-like game played with dominoes; bids go 'round, trumps are named, and small-town Southwesterners are intensely devoted to it. I have seen four men sit without moving (except to spit or scratch) for four or more hours in the pursuit of this game. One learns, generally, by watching, since no one will take off time from playing to teach it.

[23]Reprinted, with permission, from *The Livestock Weekly,* San Angelo, Texas, 10 January 1985, pp. 20-21.

[24]A typical cowboy description of such absence of beauty would go, "She's so ugly she'd have to slip up on a dipper to get a drink of water."

[25]Reprinted, with permission, from *The Livestock Weekly,* San Angelo, Texas, 9 July 1987, pp. 12-13.

Chapter Four. The Ladies, God Bless 'Em

[1]Roach, *The Cowgirls*, p. xi.

[2]Stephen Vincent Benét, *John Brown's Body* (rpt. Murray Hill, New York: Rinehart, 1955), pp. 139-40; italics added.

[3]Roach, *The Cowgirls*, pp. xiii-xv.

[4]Roach, *The Cowgirls*, p. xvi, citing "From Cowboy to Owner and Operator of Vast Domain Marked the Life of Charlie Hart," *Clovis* [New Mexico] *News Journal,* 29 May 1938, Sec. IV, p. 2.

[5]Personal interview with Deane Mansfield-Kelley, El Paso, Texas, spring 1989.

[6]Roach, *The Cowgirls,* p. 120.

[7]Kathy Kennedy, quoted in Teresa Jordan, *Cowgirls: Women of the West* (Garden City, New York: Doubleday, 1984), p. 266.

[8]Jordan, *Cowgirls,* p. 208, citing an article by George Brinton Neal in the *Boston Sunday Post,* 3 November 1935.

[9]Tad Lucas, quoted in Jordan, *Cowgirls,* pp. 204-6.

[10]Tommy J. Boley, ed., *The Autobiography of a West Texas Pioneer, Ella Elgar Bird Dumont* (Austin: University of Texas Press, 1988), pp. 103-4.

[11]Maggie Howell, quoted in Jordan, *Cowgirls,* pp. 155-57.

[12]Amy Cooksley Chubb, quoted in Jordan, *Cowgirls,* p. 9.

[13]Maggie Howell, quoted in Jordan, *Cowgirls,* p. 157.

[14]Personal interview with Deane Mansfield-Kelley, El Paso, Texas, 12 May 1989.

[15]Melody Harding, quoted in Jordan, *Cowgirls,* pp. 180, 186.

[16]Mamie Sypert Burns, *This I Can Leave You: A Woman's Days on the Pitchfork Ranch* (College Station: Texas A&M Press, 1988), pp. 107-8.

[17]Roach, *The Cowgirls,* pp. 218-19. This is noted as a "personal story," but knowing Joyce, I can't imagine that she was the "Mary" in the account.

[18]Roach, *The Cowgirls,* pp. 220-21. Again, a "personal story." I'm beginning to wonder if I know the real Joyce Roach!

[19]A note of explanation is perhaps in order for the reader's fuller understanding of Brummett's windmill story. A windmill has atop its tower a huge fan that the wind turns. (The deeper the well, the bigger the fan; a typical ranch well is about 150 feet deep, and the fan is about five to six feet in diameter.) The fan is mounted on an axle that turns a set of gears, which in turn lift and drop a long string of rods, each of which is usually twenty feet long. Called sucker rods, they are screwed together by means of connections like pipe fittings to reach the bottom of the well, which has a pipe casing of about two inches inside diameter. The bottom end of the string of sucker rods slides up and down inside a cylinder, with a set of check valves. The sucker rod has a set of leather washers, and as the washers swell with soaking up water, they fit snugly inside the cylinder, which varies in length with the depth of the well—several feet long, at least. As the sucker rod string drops into the water at the bottom of the well and strokes through the cylinder, the check valves open, letting the cylinder fill with water. When the rod is lifted, the weight of the water closes the valves and lifts the water

the length of the stroke, the water being held by the seal of the snugly fitting leathers on the sucker rod. The arrangement of valves is such that as the up-and-down motion is repeated, water is forced higher and higher until it flows out of a delivery pipe above ground level, filling the stock tank for the livestock to drink from. As the leathers (sometimes called blackjacks) wear, the seal is weakened and the pump brings up less and less water, until finally the sucker rod string has to be taken out and unscrewed, one section at a time, until the top check valve is out and the leathers can be replaced; then the procedure is reversed. The top sucker rod (called the red rod) is finally in place, the fan is reconnected, and the wind can provide lifegiving water again, until the next time.

Cowboys, who'll do anything as long as they can do it on horseback, hate windmill work. But the gears need oiling once a week or so, or their screeching can be heard for miles. Leathers wear out with the constant rubbing up and down, so they need to be replaced. Since a regular windmill man (with the proper tools) isn't always available, especially 'way out on a ranch forty miles from nowhere, the cattle's need for water must override the cowboy's lack of enthusiasm for working on windmills. While I've never greased a windmill nor changed leathers on one, reformed cowboy Richard Myers, who grew up on a ranch near Weed, New Mexico, assures me that he has had those experiences more times than he likes to remember, and my account of the leather-changing process really brought back memories, as well as being accurate. However, instead of pulling the rods by hand, as Curt and the Little Woman did, Richard would jack up a rear wheel on his pickup, bolt on a "cat head" drum in place of the wheel, and use a pulley and a rope wrapped 'round the cat head to pull the sucker rods out of the well and lower them again, the pickup engine providing the motive power. From an interview in El Paso, Texas, September 4, 1989.

[20]Curt Brummett, unpublished manuscript.

Chapter Five. Cosi—The Cowboy's Cook

[1]Adams, *Come and Get It,* p. 5. A portion of this chapter is a reworking of my article "The Galloping Gourmet, or the Chuck Wagon Cook and His Craft," in *By Land and Sea: Studies in the Folklore of Work and Leisure,* ed. Roger D. Abrahams, Kenneth S. Goldstein, and Wayland D. Hand (Hatboro, Pennsylvania: Legacy Books, 1985).

[2]Frank S. Hastings, "Some Glimpses into Ranch Life," History of Grazing in Texas, Division VI, Part A, Steps Toward Stability and Conservation, Texas Writers Project, Barker History Center, The University of Texas at Austin, unpaginated.

[3]Hastings, "Glimpses."

[4]N. Howard Thorp, "A Chuck Wagon Supper," File 5, Division 4, Folio 3, Folder 5, New Mexico Writers Project, History Library, Museum of New Mexico, Santa Fe, New Mexico. The bread-raisin-sugar pudding is essentially *capirotada,* a traditional Mexican delicacy served during Lent; Lucina L. Fischer, personal interview, El Paso, 12 December 1984. See also John O. West, *Mexican-American Folklore* (Little Rock: August House, 1988), pp. 218-19. Ernestine Sewell Linck and Joyce Gibson Roach, *Eats: A Folk History of Texas Foods* (Fort Worth: Texas Christian University Press, 1989), pp. 109-10, have sourdough recipes as well as others the chuck wagon cook would have used.

[5]Buck Kelton, interview taped by his son, Elmer Kelton, 24 October 1976, in a Brownwood, Texas, hospital. Buck was raised on the Scharbauer Ranch, and for thirty-six years lived and worked on the McElroy Ranch of Crane, Texas, where he was foreman and later manager for many years.

[6]Rod Gragg, *The Old West Quiz and Fact Book* (New York: Harper and Row, 1986), p. 121.

[7]Gragg, *Quiz and Fact Book,* p. 135.

[8]Baker, "Ft. Worth Texas Narrative."

[9]The "That's just the way I like it!" story is found all over. See Rollins, *The Cowboy,* p. 66. The biscuit story is found in Evans, *A Corral Full of Stories,* p. 48.

[10]The moose turd pie version was collected in 1954 in Maine; see J. Barre Toelken, *The Dynamics of Folklore* (Boston: Houghton Mifflin, 1979), pp. 66-67, 179-80, previously reported in West, "Galloping Gourmet," p. 219.

[11]Baker, "Ft. Worth Texas Narrative."

[12]J.J. Kalez, "Chuck Wagon Etiquette," *All Western,* undated clipping, pp. 129-30.

[13]Kalez, "Chuck Wagon Etiquette," pp. 130-31.

[14]Francis L. Fugate, "Arbuckles': The Coffee That Won the West," *American West* 21 (January-February 1984), 1: 61.

[15]Fugate, "Arbuckles'," p. 62; see also Evans, *A Corral Full of Stories,* p. 22.

[16]Rollins, *The Cowboy,* p. 66.

[17]Dedera, *Cactus Sandwich*, p. 34.

[18]Kalez, "Chuck Wagon Etiquette," p. 127.

[19]Gillett, *Six Years*, p. 26.

[20]Jean M. Burroughs, "Calf Slobber and Sonofabitch Stew," *New Mexico Magazine* (October 1988), p. 89. See also E.C. Abbott, *We Pointed Them North* (rpt. Norman: University of Oklahoma Press, 1955), p. 83; a cheap owner refused to let his hands kill a beef, and they were "supposed to live on that condemned sowbelly . . . that even the soldiers wouldn't eat"—but they killed a beef anyway!

[21]Patterson, *Sam Magoo*, p. 21.

[22]Buck Kelton interview; his recollections helped stimulate his son Elmer to write *The Good Old Boys*, of which see pp. ix-xi. Elmer sent me a copy of the tape when I was researching the chuck wagon cook.

[23]Ramírez, "Humor in Cattle Country," p. 11.

[24]Dobie, *Vaquero*, pp. 151, 152-53.

[25]Boatright, *Folk Laughter*, p. 104.

[26]John Gould, "Pie-Biter," *Coyote Wisdom* (Dallas: Southern Methodist University Press, 1938), Publications of the Texas Folklore Society 14: 185-91. See also Boatright, *Folk Laughter*, pp. 103-4.

[27]Curt Brummett, unpublished manuscript.

[28]Bob Kennon, as told to Ramon W. Adams, *From the Pecos to the Powder: A Cowboy's Autobiography* (Norman: University of Oklahoma Press, 1965), pp. 82-87.

[29]Andy Adams, *The Log of a Cowboy: A Narrative of the Old Trail Days* (Boston: Houghton Mifflin, 1903, 1931), p. 60.

[30]Ramon Adams, *Come and Get It*, p. 154.

Chapter Six. There's Something Going On Every Day

[1]Kelton, *Good Old Boys*, pp. 162-63.

[2]Dedera, *Cactus Sandwich*, pp. 41-42.

[3]Patterson, "Cowboy Comedians," pp. 105-6.

[4]Abbott, *We Pointed Them North*, p. 52.

[5]Abbott, *We Pointed Them North*, pp. 46-47.

[6]I have heard this genuine oral tale told at innumerable meetings of the Texas Folklore Society and in other wild dives, by a host of Texas tale-tellers of questionable veracity.

[7]Mark Twain, *Adventures of Huckleberry Finn* (rpt. New York: Harper and Row, 1987), chptr. 22.

[8]Hunter, *Trail Drivers*, pp. 151-52.

[9]Joseph G. McCoy, *Historic Sketches of the Cattle Trade of the West and Southwest* (rpt. Washington, D.C.: Rare Book Shop, 1932), 139-41.

[10]Abbott, *We Pointed Them North*, pp. 80-81.

[11]Abbott, *We Pointed Them North*, pp. 103-5.

[12]Benny Peacock, personal interview with Lawrence Clayton, Mussleman Ranch, 22 April 1989. Letter to the author from Lawrence Clayton, 27 April 1989.

[13]Adams, *Old-Time Cowhand.*

[14]"Jack" Thorp, "Banjo in the Cow Camps," in N. Howard "Jack" Thorp, *Songs of the Cowboys,* ed. Austin E. Fife and Alta S. Fife (New York: Clarkson N. Potter, 1966), pp. 23-24.

[15]Abbott, *We Pointed Them North*, pp. 74-75; the realism of the stories Teddy Blue told led him to note, "Why, even in *The Trail Drivers of Texas,* which is a wonderful book and absolutely authentic, you have all these old fellows telling stories, and you'd think they was a bunch of preachers, the way they talk. And yet some of them raised more hell than I did."

[16]Dedera, *Cactus Sandwich*, p. 64.

[17]Stanley Frank, reprinted by permission from *The Livestock Weekly,* San Angelo, Texas, 25 August 1960, p. 5.

[18]Abbott, *We Pointed Them North*, pp. 45-46.

[19]Stanley Frank, editor of *The Livestock Weekly,* personal letter to the author, 21 February 1989.

[20]Abbott, *We Pointed Them North*, pp. 139-40.

[21]Ramírez, "Humor in Cattle Country," p. 9.

[22]Rollins, *The Cowboy,* pp. 57-58.

[23]Abbott, *We Pointed Them North*, pp. 158-59.

[24]Paul Patterson, "Night Horse Nightmare," from a manuscript Paul typed just for me, on the back of a poster for the 1988 Texas Folklife Festival, in which he performed as a storyteller. He has related this tale—in prose—for his friends at the Texas Folklore Society on several memorable occasions.

[25]Patterson, *Pecos Tales,* p. 31.

[26]Adams, *Old-Time Cowhand,* p. 44, and Abbott, *We Pointed Them North,* p. 68, report the same story. Doubtless it was a saying that made the rounds. Abbott says that one of the trail bosses told a complaining cowhand, "You can sleep all winter in Montana."

[27]James, *27 Years*, pp. 44-45.

[28]Patterson, "Cowboy's Code," p. 43.

[29]Abbott, *We Pointed Them North,* p. 8.

[30]A nester is a settler, a sod-buster—someone who moves in to mess up good cattle range, in the waddies' view.

[31]Lee, "Legends and Folklore," pp. 50-51.

[32]Dedera, *Cactus Sandwich*, p. 62.

[33]Patterson, *Pecos Tales*, p. 19.

[34]Patterson, *Pecos Tales*, p. 44.

[35]Patterson, *Sam Magoo and Texas Too*, p. 20, and "Cowboy Comedians," p. 104. When I was a boy we had a routine that went, "Don't shoot! I'll marry your daughter. . . . Ye gods—Is that your daughter? Shoot!"

[36]C.L. Sonnichsen, telephone interview with the author, May 19, 1989.

[37]"Heifer branding" is widely reported. See Rollins, *The Cowboy*, p. 189, and Shawver and Cousins, *Chuck Wagon Windies*, p. 66.

[38]Edgar Beecher Bronson, *Cowboy Life on the Western Plains: The Reminiscences of a Ranchman* (New York: George H. Doran Co., 1910), pp. 266-73, quoted in Guy Logsdon, "The Cowboy Dance," pp. 17-21.

[39]Abbott, *We Pointed Them North*, pp. 111-13.

[40]J.R. Craddock, "The Cowboy Dance," *Coffee in the Gourd* (Austin: Texas Folklore Society, 1925), Publications of the Texas Folklore Society 2: 36.

[41]Abbott, *We Pointed Them North*, p. 37.

[42]Will C. Barnes, "The Cowboy and His Songs," *Saturday Evening Post*, 27 June 1925, p. 122. Guy Logsdon, longtime Director of Libraries at the University of Tulsa, pointed out this reference to me.

[43]Thorp, *Songs of the Cowboys* (1908), pp. 27-29; I clarified the punctuation somewhat. Note that "Santa Fe" rhymes both with "7-D" (Santa FEE) and with "say" (Santa FAY). The use of "argue," line 2, ordinarily was said as "augur" in cowboy lingo, and it meant simply to talk, chew the fat. The horse, Zebra Dun, is a frequent name for a notoriously bad horse in song and story.

[44]Thorp, *Songs of the Cowboys* (1908), pp. 17-18.

[45]Thorp, *Songs of the Cowboys* (1908), p. 20. The roofing material, "ocateo," is *ocotillo*, a tall branching cactus commonly used to cover the roofs of Mexican huts; it didn't keep out much—especially the crawling varmints of the Southwest. The song was written to be sung to the tune of a popular frontier song, "The Little Old Log Cabin in the Lane," which also furnished the tune for Thorp's immortal "Little Joe the Wrangler." See Thorp, *Songs of the Cowboys* (1966), pp. 28-30 and 87-89.

[46]Rollins, *The Cowboy*, pp. 174-75.

[47]Thorp, *Songs of the Cowboys* (1908), pp. 33-36; in N. Howard Thorp, *Songs of the Cowboys* (Boston: Houghton Mifflin, 1921), p. 35, he reported his source, and accepted Chittenden as the presumed author of the original poem. See John O. West, "Jack Thorp and John Lomax," pp. 113-18, Connie Ricci, "The Cowboy's Christmas Ball: The Historicity of a Cowboy Ballad," *Sonofagun Stew* (Dallas: Southern Methodist University Press, 1985), Publications of the Texas Folklore Society 46: 28-35, and the 1966 edition of *Songs of the Cowboy*, pp. 219-20.

[48]Ramírez, "Humor in Cattle Country," pp. 3-4.

[49]Nancy Patterson, "Johnny Tulk: A Man and His Humor," unpublished manuscript in the University of Texas at El Paso Folklore Archive, pp. 7-9. A rider, on bareback or saddle bronc, is judged in part by how hard the horse bucks; if a horse "jackrabbits"—just jumps around with no attempt at unhorsing the rider—he can't make a very good score.

[50]Abbott, *We Pointed Them North*, pp. 124-25. Teddy Blue gives the recipe for Indian whiskey, which—if taken seriously—may help explain its power: "You take one barrel of Missouri River water and two gallons of alcohol. Then you add two ounces of strychnine to make them crazy—because strychnine is the greatest stimulant in the world—and three plugs of chewing tobacco to make them sick—because an Indian wouldn't figure it was whiskey unless it made him sick—and five bars of soap to give it a bead, and half a pound of red pepper, and then you put in some sagebrush and boil it until it's brown. Strain this into a barrel and you've got your Indian whiskey, that one bottle calls for one buffalo robe, and when the Indian got drunk it was two robes. And that's how some of the traders made their fortune" (pp. 123-24).

Chapter Seven. Cowboys Do the Damnedest Things

[1]Kelton, *Good Old Boys*, pp. 176-77. A "dally"—from the Spanish *dar la vuelta*—to take a turn (around the saddle horn)—is a standard cowboy term. "Take a wrap" has the same function.

[2]Thorp, *Songs of the Cowboys* (1921), pp. 81-83. A number of small alterations, omissions, and transpositions are found here, confirming the fact that Thorp wrote the song down from a recitation or presentation in song, and not from the original poem. "Mokiones" is an attempt at writing the usual pronunciation for Mogollones, a

mountainous region of western New Mexico; "muggy yones" comes pretty close. The original appears in Charles Badger Clark, *Sun and Saddle Leather* (rpt. Stockton, California: Westerners Foundation, 1962), pp. 77-80. John I. White, in *Git Along Little Dogies*, pp. 126-36, discusses Badger Clark and "High-Chin Bob." The song/story also carries the title "The Glory Trail" in Mabel Major and T.M. Pearce, *Signature of the Sun: Southwest Verse, 1900-1950* (Albuquerque: University of New Mexico Press, 1950), pp. 103-5, where I first read it. Some ropers generally "took a dally" and could let go; High-Chin Bob, although he was not a "tie-fast" man, couldn't release the rope from the saddle horn because his "sinful pride" wouldn't let him.

[3]Curt Brummett, unpublished manuscript.

[4]Barbara Fox, quoted in Teresa Jordan, *Cowgirls: Women of the American West* (Garden City, New York: Doubleday, 1984), pp. 66-67.

[5]Roach, *The Cowgirls*, pp. 57-58, citing Ann Bassett Willis, "Queen Ann of Brown's Park," *Colorado Magazine* 29 (June 1952): 233-35.

[6]Dobie, *Vaquero*, pp. 171-72.

[7]Dobie, *Vaquero*, pp. 242-43.

[8]Adams, *Old-Time Cowhand*, p. 41.

[9]Patterson, "Cowboy Comedians," p. 102.

[10]Dobie, *Vaquero*, pp. 240-41.

[11]Rollins, *The Cowboy*, pp. 183-84.

[12]Col. Bailey C. Haines, *Bill Pickett, Bulldogger: The Biography of a Black Cowboy* (Norman: University of Oklahoma Press, 1977), pp. 26-27, 65-181. Ray Past, "Brown Men on Horseback," *Negro Digest* 6.3 (January 1948): 31-34, estimates from a study of cattle trail materials that some six thousand blacks took part in the cattle-drives, and that there was no "racial problem" on the trail. If a man did his job, then he was a man. Several black cowboys, like Pickett, were quite well-known in those days.

[13]Haines, *Bill Pickett*, p. 186.

[14]Patterson, "Cowboy Comedians," p. 103; a similar story is in Dedera, *Cactus Sandwich*, p. 44.

[15]Dedera, *Cactus Sandwich*, p. 63.

[16]Lee, "Legends and Folklore," pp. 115-16. She collected the story during an interview with a relative, Joseph Bee Handley.

References

Adams, Andy. *The Log of a Cowboy: A Narrative of the Old Trail Days*. Boston: Houghton Mifflin, 1903, 1931.

Adams, Ramon F. *Come and Get It: The Story of the Old Cowboy Cook*. Norman: University of Oklahoma Press, 1952.

------. *The Old-Time Cowhand*. New York: Macmillan, 1961.

Abbott, E.C. *We Pointed Them North*. Rpt. Norman: University of Oklahoma Press, 1955.

Anderson, Ronnie. Interview with the author, El Paso, Texas, 27 January 1989.

Baker, John J. "Fort Worth Texas Narrative," Fort Worth History Notes, Folder 68: Interviews, Texas Writers Project, Barker History Center, The University of Texas at Austin, 26830.

Barnes, Will C. "The Cowboy and His Songs." *Saturday Evening Post,* 27 June 1925, p. 122.

Boatright, Mody C. Class lectures, "Southwestern Life and Literature," The University of Texas, June 1962.

------. *Folk Laughter on the American Frontier.* New York: Collier Books, 1961.

------. *Tall Tales from Texas Cow Camps.* Rpt. Dallas: Southern Methodist University Press, 1982.

Boley, Tommy J., ed. *An Autobiography of a West Texas Pioneer, Ella Elgar Bird Dumont.* Austin: University of Texas Press, 1988.

Botkin, Benjamin A. *A Treasury of Western Folklore.* New York: Crown, 1951.

Bratcher, James D. "The Baby-Switching Story." *The Sunny Slopes of Long Ago* (Dallas: Southern Methodist University Press, 1966), Publications of the Texas Folklore Society 33: 110-17.

Brummett, Curt. Unpublished manuscripts.

Clark, Charles Badger. *Sun and Saddle Leather.* Rpt. Stockton, California: Westerners Foundation, 1962.

Clayton, Lawrence. Letter to the author, 27 April 1989.

------. "The Mounted Herdsmen of the West: Regional Variation—the Vaquero, Cowboy, and Buckaroo," unpublished manuscript.

Craddock, J.R. "The Cowboy Dance." *Coffee in the Gourd* (Austin: Texas Folklore Society, 1925), Publications of the Texas Folklore Society 2: 36.

Dedera, Don. *The Cactus Sandwich and Other Tall Tales of the Southwest.* Flagstaff, Arizona: Northland Press, 1986.

Dobie, J. Frank. *The Longhorns.* New York: Bramhall House, 1941.

------. "Mustang Gray: Fact, Tradition, and Song," in *Tone the Bell Easy* (Dallas: Southern Methodist University Press, 1932), Publications of the Texas Folklore Society 10: 109-11.

------. *Rattlesnakes.* Rpt. Austin: University of Texas Press, 1982.

------. *A Vaquero of the Brush Country.* Boston: Little, Brown, 1943.

Duval, John C. *The Adventures of Big-Foot Wallace, the Texas Ranger and Hunter.* Macon, Georgia: J.W. Burke, 1870.

Erickson, John R. *Cowboys Are Partly Human.* Perryton, Texas: Maverick Books, 1983.

------. "Language of the Cow Camp Has Flavor All Its Own." *Prorodeo Sports News* (27 June 1979): 23-24.

Evans, Joe. *A Corral Full of Stories.* El Paso: McMath, 1939.

Flynt, Bill Walton. Interview with the author, c. 1936.

Folk Tales from the Patagonia Area, Santa Cruz County, Arizona, University of Arizona Bulletin, General Bulletin No. 13, 19: 4 (October 1948). Quoted in Benjamin A. Botkin, *A Treasury of Western Folklore.* New York: Crown, 1951.

Gillett, James B. *Six Years with the Texas Rangers.* Rpt. Lincoln: University of Nebraska Press, 1976.

Gillis, Everett. "Weather Talk from the Caprock." *Folk Travelers* (Dallas: Southern Methodist University Press, 1953), Publications of the Texas Folklore Society 25: 200.

Gragg, Rod. *The Old West Quiz and Fact Book.* New York: Harper and Row, 1986.

Haines, Col. Bailey C. *Bill Pickett, Bulldogger: The Biography of a Black Cowboy.* Norman: University of Oklahoma Press, 1977.

Harris, Stanley W. "Stories of Ranch People." *Singers and Storytellers* (Dallas: Southern Methodist University Press, 1961), Publications of the Texas Folklore Society 30: 176.

Hunter, J. Marvin, ed. *The Trail Drivers of Texas.* N.p.: The Old Trail Drivers Association, 1920.

James, Will S. *27 Years a Maverick, or Life on the Texas Range.* Rpt. Austin: Steck-Vaughn Co., 1968.

Jordan, Teresa. *Cowgirls: Women of the American West.* Garden City, New York: Doubleday, 1984.

Kelton, Buck. Interview with Elmer Kelton, Brownwood, Texas, 24

October 1976.

Kelton, Elmer. *The Good Old Boys.* Rpt. Fort Worth: Texas Christian University Press, 1985.

------. Interview with the author, Uvalde, Texas, 23 March 1989.

------. Letter to the author, January 18, 1989.

Kennon, Bob, as told to Ramon W. Adams. *From the Pecos to the Powder: A Cowboy's Autobiography.* Norman: University of Oklahoma Press, 1965.

Lee, Martha Faye Handley. "Legends and Folklore of the Greenbelt of the Texas Panhandle." Master's thesis, University of Texas at El Paso, 1969.

Linck, Ernestine Sewell, and Joyce Gibson Roach. *Eats: A Folk History of Texas Foods.* Fort Worth: Texas Christian University Press, 1989.

Logsdon, Guy. "The Cowboy Dance: From Ranch House to Road House." Unpublished manuscript.

------. *The Whorehouse Bells Are Ringing.* Urbana: University of Illinois Press, 1989.

Lomax, John A. *Cowboy Songs and Other Frontier Ballads.* New York: Macmillan, 1920.

Major, Mabel, and T.M. Pearce, *Signature of the Sun: Southwest*

Verse, 1900-1950. Albuquerque: University of New Mexico Press, 1950.

Mansfield-Kelley, Deane. Interview with the author, El Paso, Texas, spring 1989.

McDowell, Bart. *The American Cowboy in Life and Legend.* Washington, D.C.: National Geographic Society, 1972.

Myers, Richard. Interview with the author, El Paso, Texas, September 4, 1989.

Ohrlin, Glenn. *The Hell-Bound Train: A Cowboy Songbook.* Urbana: University of Illinois Press, 1973.

Past, Ray. "Brown Men on Horseback." *Negro Digest* 6.3 (January 1948): 31-34.

Patterson, Nancy. "Johnny Tulk: A Man and His Humor," unpublished manuscript in the University of Texas at El Paso Folklore Archive.

Patterson, Paul. "The Cowboy's Code." *The Sunny Slopes of Long Ago* (Dallas: Southern Methodist University Press, 1966), Publications of the Texas Folklore Society 33: 42-44.

------. "Cowboy Comedians and Horseback Humorists." *The Golden Log* (Dallas: Southern Methodist University Press, 1962), Publications of the Texas Folklore Society 31: 105-6.

------. *Crazy Women in the Rafters: Memories of a Texas Boyhood.* Norman: University of Oklahoma Press, 1976.

-----. Interview with the author, Uvalde, Texas, 23 March 1989.

-----. "Night Horse Nightmare," unpublished manuscript.

-----. *Pecos Tales.* Austin: Texas Folklore Society, 1967.

-----. *Sam Magoo and Texas Too.* Dallas: Mathis, Van Nort, & Co., 1947.

"Pecos Bill." In *Melody Time.* Walt Disney Productions, c. 1954.

Ramírez, Nora. "Humor in Cattle Country." Unpublished manuscript in the University of Texas at El Paso Folklore Archive.

Roach, Joyce Gibson. *The Cowgirls.* Houston: Cordovan Corp., 1978.

Rollins, Philip A. *The Cowboy.* New York: Charles Scribner's Sons, 1922.

Scudday, Roy. "The Musical Snake." *From Hell to Breakfast* (Dallas: Southern Methodist University Press, 1944), Publications of the Texas Folklore Society 19: 162-64.

Shawver, Lora, and Walt Cousins. *Chuck Wagon Windies and Range Poems.* San Antonio: Naylor, 1934.

Sonnichsen, C.L. *Cowboys and Cattle Kings: Life on the Range Today.* Rpt. Westport, Connecticut: Greenwood Press, 1980.

------. *The Laughing West.* Athens, Ohio: Swallow Press/Ohio University Press, 1988.

------. Telephone interview with the author, May 19, 1989.

Steinbeck, John. *Tortilla Flat.* New York: Viking, 1963.

Tarkington, Booth. *Penrod.* New York: Grossett and Dunlap, 1914.

"Texas Girl Captures Lion with Lasso," undated clipping from unnamed newspaper in the Western History Collection, Denver Public Library. Quoted in Joyce Gibson Roach, *The Cowgirls.* Houston: Cordovan Corp., 1978.

Thorp, N. Howard. *Songs of the Cowboys.* Estancia, New Mexico: News Print Shop, 1908.

------. *Songs of the Cowboys.* Boston: Houghton Mifflin, 1921.

Thorp, N. Howard "Jack." *Songs of the Cowboys.* Ed. Austin E. and Alta S. Fife. New York: Clarkson N. Potter, 1966.

West, John O. "Billy the Kid: Hired Gun or Hero?" *The Sunny Slopes of Long Ago* (Dallas: Southern Methodist University Press, 1966), Publications of the Texas Folklore Society 33: 70-80.

------. "The Galloping Gourmet, or The Chuck Wagon Cook and His Craft." In *By Land and Sea: Studies in the Folklore of Work and Leisure,* ed. Roger D. Abrahams, Kenneth S. Goldstein, and Wayland D. Hand. Hatboro, Pennsylvania: Legacy Books, 1985.

------. "Jack Thorp and John Lomax: Oral or Written Transmission?" *Western Folklore* 26.2 (April 1967): 113-18.

------. *Mexican-American Folklore.* Little Rock: August House, 1988.

White, John I. *Git Along Little Dogies: Songs and Songmakers of the American West.* Urbana: University of Illinois Press, 1975.

Willis, Ann Bassett. "Queen Ann of Brown's Park." *Colorado Magazine* 29 (June 1952): 233-35.

Wister, Owen. *The Virginian.* New York: Macmillan, 1902.

JOHN O. WEST (it's not a pseudonym, and the O. doesn't stand for Old) is the author of *Mexican-American Folklore* and numerous other publications on Southwestern culture. A professor of English at the University of Texas at El Paso, he lives in El Paso with his wife, Lucy, and son, Johnny.